Literature & Landscape

Literature & Landscape

Writers of the Southwest

Cynthia Farah

Copyright © 1988
Texas Western Press
The University of Texas at El Paso
El Paso, Texas 79968-0633

All rights reserved. No part of this book may be used or reproduced in any manner without the written permission of Texas Western Press, except in the case of brief quotations employed in reviews and similar critical work.

The excerpt from *Our Southwest* by Erna Fergusson is published with permission of Alfred A. Knopf, Inc.

First Edition
Library of Congress Catalog Card 88-050546
ISBN 87404-206-2

The paper used in this publication meets the minimum requirements of American National Standard for Information Sciences — Permanence of Paper for Printed Library Materials, ANSI Z39.48-1984. ∞

Contents

xi **Preface**

The Writers

2 Edward Abbey
4 Lee K. Abbott
6 Rudolfo A. Anaya
8 Byrd Baylor
10 Elroy Bode
12 Richard Bradford
14 Ernest J. Burrus, S.J.
16 Fray Angélico Chávez
18 Denise Chávez
20 Peggy Pond Church
22 William Eastlake
24 Max Evans
26 Floyd S. Fierman
28 Bernard Fontana
30 Gene Frumkin
32 Joy Harjo
34 Tony Hillerman
36 Rolando Hinojosa-Smith
38 Paul Horgan
40 Dorothy B. Hughes
42 Arturo Islas
44 Elmer Kelton
46 David Lavender
48 Tom Lea
50 Harold Littlebird

52 Mark Medoff
54 Leon C. Metz
56 N. Scott Momaday
58 Pat Mora
60 Gary Paul Nabhan
62 John Nichols
64 Stanley Noyes
66 Lawrence Clark Powell
68 Jim Sagel
70 Ricardo Sánchez
72 Jack Schaefer
74 Marc Simmons
76 John L. Sinclair
78 Joseph Somoza
80 C.L. Sonnichsen
82 Stan Steiner
84 Elizabeth Tallent
86 Luci Tapahonso
88 Sabine R. Ulibarrí
90 Frank Waters
92 Marta Weigle
94 Jeanne Williams
96 Keith Wilson
98 Norman Zollinger
100 Ann Zwinger

Lives and Works

105 Edward Abbey
105 Lee K. Abbott
106 Rudolfo A. Anaya
106 Byrd Baylor
107 Elroy Bode
107 Richard Bradford
108 Ernest J. Burrus, S.J.
109 Fray Angélico Chávez
110 Denise Chávez
111 Peggy Pond Church
111 William Eastlake
112 Max Evans
112 Floyd S. Fierman
113 Bernard Fontana
114 Gene Frumkin
114 Joy Harjo
115 Tony Hillerman
115 Rolando Hinojosa-Smith
116 Paul Horgan
117 Dorothy B. Hughes
118 Arturo Islas
118 Elmer Kelton
119 David Lavender
120 Tom Lea
121 Harold Littlebird
121 Mark Medoff
122 Leon C. Metz
123 N. Scott Momaday
123 Pat Mora
124 Gary Paul Nabhan
124 John Nichols
125 Stanley Noyes
125 Lawrence Clark Powell
126 Jim Sagel
127 Ricardo Sánchez
127 Jack Schaefer
128 Marc Simmons
129 John L. Sinclair
129 Joseph Somoza
130 C.L. Sonnichsen
131 Stan Steiner
131 Elizabeth Tallent
132 Luci Tapahonso
132 Sabine R. Ulibarrí
133 Frank Waters
134 Marta Weigle
134 Jeanne Williams
136 Keith Wilson
136 Norman Zollinger
137 Ann Zwinger

The arid Southwest has always been too strong, too indomitable for most people. Those who can stand it have had to learn that man does not modify this country; it transforms him, deeply. Perhaps our generation will come to appreciate it as the country God remembered and saved for man's delight when he could mature enough to understand it. God armored it, as the migrating Easterner learned in his anguish, with thorns on the trees, stings and horns on the bugs and beasts. He fortified it with mountain ranges and trackless deserts. He filled it with such hazards as no legendary hero ever had to surmount. The Southwest can never be remade into a landscape that produces bread and butter. But it is infinitely productive of the imponderables so much needed by a world weary of getting and spending. It is wilderness where a man may get back to the essentials of being a man. It is magnificence forever rewarding to a man courageous enough to seek to renew his soul.

Erna Fergusson (1888-1964)
(From *Our Southwest.*
New York: Knopf, 1940.)

Preface

The creation of *Literature and Landscape: Writers of the Southwest* has been a labor of love, my love for a special place and for the talent of those who can creatively express their feelings about the American Southwest.

The El Paso Public Library initially provided the inspiration for the book. I wanted to present a gift to the institution which had introduced me, at a very early age, to worlds past, present and future, worlds presented in books. Years later, I realized that I truly had not explored my own backyard, the Southwest. Returning from college and other adventures, I finally understood that the desert was not the end of the earth. It was the beginning of many special experiences.

Mary Sarber, head of the Southwest Collection at the El Paso Public Library, proved to be the perfect guide. She had a serious interest in my field of photography and an encyclopedic knowledge of Southwestern literature. After some discussion, we decided that I should create a photographic document of the important authors who were living in and writing about the Southwest, and present those prints to the library.

Mary compiled a list of several dozen writers, most of whom I did not recognize. She introduced me to bibliographic guides written by her mentor Lawrence Clark Powell. I then became acquainted with my photographic subjects by sitting down with their books. The enthusiasm and excitement grew as I read William Eastlake's *Go In Beauty*, Tom Lea's *The Wonderful Country*, Richard Bradford's *Red Sky At Morning*. These people were able to put into words the feelings I had for the Southwest.

I began playing detective in earnest. Limits had to be set or there would be no end to the project. The Southwest was defined as Arizona, New Mexico, and West Texas. Authors selected had to have published several creative works of fiction or nonfiction. Local historians and most academics were omitted.

Writers are very private people. Theirs is a very solitary profession. But mention a project for a public library, and they are willing to participate without hesitation.

The next four years were spent exploring the Southwest in pursuit of writers' images. I followed hand-drawn maps to Marc Simmons' camp in the desert near Cerrillos, New Mexico. Although born one hundred years too late, he has managed to recreate, in his adobe compound, an era when phones were nonexistent and when a farrier was an honored professional. His concessions to the twentieth century are a manual typewriter and a library any university would envy.

Peggy Pond Church graciously invited me to her home in Santa Fe which was surrounded by bushes and birds. She served tea and lamented her failing senses and her inability to maintain such a large home. The last time we met was in her apartment, which she found too confining and where she chose to overcome her "addiction to life."

I followed John Nichols in his truck over dirt roads in Taos as he yelled greetings in Spanish to local farmers. Awaiting him at his small farmhouse was a call from his agent concerning John's increasing success as a screenwriter. A social revolutionary in Hollywood can be a dichotomy. John can handle the pressure.

My subjects were not particularly vain people, as demonstrated by their repeated use of outdated pictures on the dust jackets of their books. Seeing them in person was often a pleasant surprise. I was curious to see what they looked like, just as I hope you are.

Those updated, current images finally became a photography exhibit which debuted in the Lea-Hertzog room of the El Paso Public Library. But a permanent document was needed, in the form of a sourcebook for students, readers, teachers, and collectors of books. It could be used as a guide and an introduction to writers who have enriched many lives and helped many "acknowledge the wonder."

All of the writers I had photographed were recontacted to verify and update for this book biographical and bibliographical information. Each author was asked to answer the question: "What role has the Southwestern landscape played in compelling you to write?" Virtually everyone responded with an original, previously unpublished comment. The answers range from humorous to profound. They are all insightful.

It was extremely difficult to decide whom to include and whom to exclude. Which writers would endure and which become obscure? I relied on the advice of several experts in compiling the final list. A concerted effort was made to make it as comprehensive as possible.

As the publishing deadline approached, it became obvious that the Southwest and Southwestern authors were almost impossible to categorize. The final choice of fifty writers became a very subjective list. I thought it important to include several more authors who wrote great books based in the Southwest, but who lived outside my arbitrary boundary. The landscape bordering Texas and Mexico, a land all too often overlooked, took on greater significance on my map.

I am very much aware that compiling such a book cannot be done without injustice. Ultimately, however, the purpose of this project is to recognize and honor fifty very special people, pioneers and rising stars. They write mysteries, histories, children's books, love stories, and poems which happen to be set in the Southwest. They are American writers, just as Faulkner, London, and Steinbeck were American writers whose talents evolved from a strong sense of place.

The Writers

Edward Abbey

I would have been a writer wherever I lived, but the deserts, mountains, rivers, and canyons of the American Southwest have been my home and spiritual center since I first saw them in 1944. In that sense, the landscape has been a part of my writing, as of my life, for more than forty years.

Lee K. Abbott

Whenever I am asked what it means to be a Southern writer, I rise up on my high horse, as my father said the aggrieved ought to do, and insist that I am, if these distinctions matter at all, a Southwestern writer. By which I mean to put in the minds of the curious a picture of Disney-worthy color and dimension: vistas and Martian-like scrub, high heavens and sterile New Mexico deserts that go yonder forever. I mean for the keen to see mountains like organ pipes, a Rio Grande wet in spring only, and, moving upon that mostly rural world, a loud, Jeep-happy, jean-clad population with names like Jim Bob and April May Rains (honest).

The truth is that until 1979 I had no voice, least of all a Southwestern one. Instead, I had that voice (in the lies I published and the life I led) you can hear from the time-weather folks — dispassionate as a toddler's "Speak and Spell," what a Chrysler says when its door's ajar. But that year I went umpteen hours by Amtrak and four more by Greyhound to visit my father in Las Cruces after he'd sold our house to take up the bluehearted life of a retiree. So it was in my weeks there, the Town & Country apartments off Desert Drive behind the Apodaca Park baseball diamonds I'd played Little League on, that I came to my writer's decision: I am a shitkicker.

Voice — which has something to do with character and spirit, custom and practice, habit and morality — is a function of place. Its authority comes from the crossroads where you learned what you know. And in 1979 I understood that all I knew, and could therefore type about, was Heibert's Drive-In, the Pit Stop where rock and roll was learned, the rivalry our country club had with the Elks' version of gentility, skiing on the irrigation canals, skinny-dipping at the flumes — all given meaning by the chitchat they were lived in.

Rudolfo A. Anaya

In speaking about landscape, I would prefer to use the Spanish word *la tierra,* simply because it conveys a deeper relationship between man and his place, and it is this kinship to the environment which creates the metaphor and the epiphany in landscape. On one pole of the metaphor stands man — on the other is the raw, majestic, and awe-inspiring landscape of the Southwest; the epiphany is the natural response to that landscape, a coming together of these two forces. And because I feel a close kinship with my environment, I feel constantly in touch with that epiphany which opens me up to receive the power in my landscape.

I don't believe a person can be born and raised in the Southwest and not be affected by the land. The landscape changes the man, and the man becomes his landscape. My earliest memories were molded by the forces in my landscape: sun, wind, rain, the llano, the river. And all of these forces were working to create the people that walked across my plane of vision. And my vision was limited until I was taught to see the stark beauty which surrounded me. I was fortunate to meet a few, old ancianos who taught me to respond to my landscape and to acquire the harmony which is inherent between man and his place.

Byrd Baylor

    Maybe everybody has some small part of the world where they feel most at home, some place that comforts them and holds them. The Southwestern desert is like that for me. I feel at home with cliffs and mesa and rocks and open skies. I'm comforted by desert storms. I want to know the things that hawks and horned toads know. I want to understand dust devils and falling stars. I want to follow coyote trails wherever they go. I like to talk to people who remember sunsets that they saw five years ago, and to people who can tell you all about a certain purple cactus flower that they walk across a mountain every spring to find. Of course the desert keeps its secrets hidden and only lets you in on a few of them, but I learn what I can, and that is what I write about. All my books are full of places and people I know. I think of them as my own kind of private love songs to my own part of the world.

Elroy Bode

When I think of the Southwest, I think of the pleasures of Saturday afternoon: of side roads above Las Cruces, in early fall, that go past cottonwoods and canals. I think of wide fields at two o'clock in quietly spacious New Mexico at two o'clock.

I have never been where the sun is such a steady friend of the earth and touches it so serenely. Yet at times I almost hurt from the physical drama of sky-and-land. Every surface is sharp and I almost cut myself on air.

Sometimes the land is moody: I like the smoky, sun-lit sweep of mountains stretching across the horizon near Alamogordo, with plumes of dust devils rising from the desert floor like random campfires and summer clouds casting their great patches of shade.

I say this: Give me a crossroads adobe building on the road from El Paso to Old Mesilla, an apple box to sit on, the sun above the dunes to the west and the Franklins to my back: Give me that stretch of ground and I will have all of eternity that I will ever need.

Richard Bradford

You know those bleached cows' skulls that Georgia O'Keeffe used to paint? Well, the Southwestern landscape is littered with them, and whenever I see one, I think: "Bradford, if you don't get something published pretty soon, you're going to end up like that."

Ernest J. Burrus, S.J.

The limitless deserts seem to reflect the infinity of God which I had pondered over so many times. Even the historical maps which I felt inspired to reproduce and study in several volumes are really "microlandscapes" of manageable size and dimensions that help us understand the larger and gigantic reality.

When I read the writings of others — explorers, missionaries, pioneer settlers — I could thrill to their reaction and share their experience, so similar to mine but also different, infinitely nuanced, often profounder than mine because elicited by those who lived in calmer and more reflective times. I wanted others to share their knowledge, their enthusiasm and intense emotions as recorded centuries ago and lived through the years. I could not but write and thus share their precious treasures.

Above all, it was the people living in and acting on the vast stage we call the Southwest that inspired me to write. Their visions, their prophecies, their hopes, their tragedies, their forebodings, their successes and failures — these are the themes of all my books, whether in the reproduction of historic texts or in the presentation of original compositions.

Fray Angélico Chávez

What compelled me to write poetry and prose fiction from my earliest days was my love for English literature. Naturally, our landscape came in as the background. In historical research, my aim was to clarify or correct my Hispanic and Franciscan heritage.

Denise Chávez

I was born in Las Cruces, New Mexico, in a time of extreme heat, in August. Since then, I have carried that heat with me, wherever I have lived. A sensitivity to heat, a release in rain, these are my earliest memories. I cannot go outside without seeing the Organ Mountains. Everywhere I have lived, I have been in a proximity to mountains. To me, the mountains symbolize the strength of enduring love/loves. The sky is a part of my interior/exterior world, it is the ceiling of my dreams, my world horizon. The change of seasons, so subtle in the south, has occasioned many an observation from me, and has found its expression in my writing.

I feel as if I am New Mexico, as well as Texas, my mother's home place. I am a combined world of heat and dust and little rain. I like, more than like, love to write about the people of this world, the compadres and comadres I have grown up with, the maids I have loved, who've taken care of me, taught me the language of love, the handymen who left their indelible mark of kindness in my heart.

I recall the heat, the still nights, the sound of the train from the track at the end of the block; feel the approaching storm; have wandered in the weeds and the dust; have cried and laughed in the gentle rain or in the swirling dust. I am a child of the south, a child of heat, a child of the mountains. I understand what it is to feel joy in snow, ecstasy in rain, wonder in storms, and to feel the eternal quiet of the sunset or the early morning in an empty, almost empty field, where only the ants and insects and the small animals live. To understand me is to know this land I love.

Peggy Pond Church

   I am fortunate to have been surrounded most of my life by the great rhythms of light and shadow that move over the arid New Mexico landscape. The tension between heights and depths in mountain and mesa, the seasonal movement of stars and weathers, the exposures of geologic time, these seem to call forth in all my senses resonances with music and poetry which influence not only the substance but the structure of all my writing, whether in prose or verse. I became hooked at an early age — not quite thirteen, to be exact — on trying to put the landscape into words; compelled is exactly the right word. Even personal emotion has often been felt in terms of landforms, the inner drama projected into the drama of the natural world around me, or the natural world reflected by the inner.

   The essence of the New Mexico landscape is what it does with light, from the flash of color on sky-touched mountains to the facets of crystal sandgrains in a dry arroyo. Light — and the great visible rhythms of time — by these I have been surrounded, in these I have felt myself rooted for the greater part of a lifetime.

William Eastlake

The landscape has played an important part in my Southwest novels, as in the opening of *Go in Beauty:* "Once upon a time there was time. The land here in the Southwest had evolved slowly and there was time and there were great spaces. Now a man on horseback from atop a bold mesa looked out over the violent spectrum of the Indian Country — into a gaudy infinity where all the colors of the world exploded, soundlessly. 'There's not much time,' he said."

Max Evans

I have an Indian feeling towards the land; if you want to call that a religion it's fine by me. We are the land, that's all. You can't hide it in concrete, plastic or cocaine, it still gets to us all. Today I stopped in a gas station and the first words voiced after "fill 'er up" were about the weather. It was the same at the drugstore when I paid for the paper, and when I got home my wife said, "I was going to paint, but who can stay indoors on a day like this." I don't care if you're on Sunset Boulevard, Fifth Avenue, or the Cervantes Bar in Albuquerque, New Mexico, at least twenty-five percent of the conversation winds up about the elements.

In writing I suppose the people come first because that's the part of the land you and I are. But the elements influence forcefully all of life here. After long, high winds, violence rises. Heated steaming summers have instigated far-reaching and deadly riots and unleashed tragically repressed passions. No matter how expertly, when a writer writes just of the society of people, he's only reaching half way home. Hell, old Shakespeare himself never did get far from that little green river. Eat the dirt, drink the blood, push the ink, watch the coyote steal a chicken for its young, and if it's in you — out it'll come.

Floyd S. Fierman

The Western pioneer, like the Biblical Psalmist, was shaped by his environment. To come from verdant terrain with all its rain, to stark desert and barren mountains can arouse either inspiration or depression. When the Psalmist wrote, "I lift mine eyes unto the mountains, whence cometh my help," I believe that he was depressed rather than inspired. He was asking God for assistance. He answered himself: "My help cometh from the Lord who made the heavens and the earth."

When I was drawn to the Southwest, I first accustomed mine eyes to look at the piñon tree, the yucca, and the saguaro. I had lived the formative years of my life in Ohio and Pennsylvania, where the oak, the elm, and the maple trees grow, and this ambience was different from that in the Southwest. With this orientation I had direction. This was a new adventure. The glare and the shadows of bare mountains tell you something that verdant landscapes and concrete forests cannot relate.

At first I was lonely and sometimes I still feel isolated, alone. Water is precious, fuel is costly, public parks in which to picnic, rare, and wealth is king. The poverty around me sickens me. But this has given me a goal, not only to tell the story of the People of the Book and The Brook, "the people who wept by the waters of Babylon," but also the story of people who live in mud huts, have little food, many children, and who sing "La Cucaracha," about the cockroach who, uninvited, shares the dwelling. It is my uplifted head looking at the rocky mountains that urges me: Relate the story! Write the legend! Imitate the Psalmist!

Bernard Fontana

It is not the Southwestern landscape that has compelled me to write. I began writing in elementary school, growing up in the Sacramento Valley of California, and I have never stopped writing.

The Southwestern landscape has certainly entered into everything I've written since living in the Southwest beginning in 1955. But "landscape" includes the cultural landscape as well as the physical one; indeed, they are the history and culture of the region. It is how these have inescapably been affected by the environment, that has attracted my interest. And "interest" is too mild a word.

The focus of my writing is people, people in a special place, people who are both wounded and healed by the circumstances of the landscape in which they find themselves.

What is incredible about the Southwestern landscape is its openness. Its vistas, both horizontally and vertically, are unobstructed. And just as one can see the stratigraphy of colored rocks, so can one see the layers of human succession. The rocks remain; so do all of us who have viewed them.

Gene Frumkin

Since I was born in New York City and lived there my first ten years, then lived in Los Angeles for more than twenty-five years, I experienced a heavy urban background before moving to Albuquerque in 1966. Although Albuquerque is a city, for me it was a very small one and, besides, one could leave it for the open country in ten minutes. So the impact on me originally was heavy.

I was awestruck, really, by the open spaces and the huge sky. These were not old facts to me, but quite fresh ones. In Los Angeles, where I first began writing poetry and some fiction, I had much difficulty in depicting place. I wanted to deal, in some ways, with the places my experience had given me, but I couldn't. In some fourteen years I probably centered only about five poems on Los Angeles or New York as a place.

After coming to New Mexico, the elements of nature, the new look at it, gave me numerous poems. They just kept coming.... Some fiction I have written and published also has New Mexico as a factor in one way or another.

These works are a product of something larger: a wholly different outlook on life and my place in it. Even when the Southwest region is not directly involved in a given work, or a collection, it is nevertheless in some manner there because for me where I am is a strong element in what and how I write.... It's the Southwest with which I most identify. It's the best place, the most creatively stimulating, that I have ever found to live in.

Joy Harjo

The compelling spirit, or at least a powerful and recognizable force behind what I write, is certainly the Southwestern landscape. This is not in vague or romantic terms, but tangible as the scarlet cliff rise that signals the beginning of Jemez country, when you are looking from way off, and driving in from Albuquerque or someplace else south. I carried a photograph of that place until it nearly disintegrated, but that's not particularly important because that place lives behind every word I ever write, if I am being honest to what I know, where I have been, to what I am becoming. And that place is multiplied by others in my memory, in Oklahoma, other areas in New Mexico, Arizona.... Wherever I write, I stand in this beautiful and bittersweet country, the land that triggered the curious and terrifying place within me that forces me to write.

Tony Hillerman

From the first time I experienced it, the landscape of the Southern Rockies has moved me. I think I could never be happy for long away from a place where I can see mountains on the horizon, the great sky overhead, and the sense of "room enough and time" which the high desert gives me.

It seems to me that this big desert country puts man in a different perspective than does the green, fertile, hospitable flatlands of middle America — or the gentle mountains of the east. And of course the inhabitants ARE different in subtle ways. Add all this together and somehow it makes me want to write about it.

Rolando Hinojosa-Smith

The Southwest figures prominently, exclusively almost, in all of my work, and with particular reference to the people since it is people who make the history of a place.

The cross-cultural ties in my life are inescapable, and these, too, are easy to evince in all of the writing. And to such an extent that I've written several novels in Spanish and then gone back to re-create them in English; e.g., *Estampas* became *The Valley, Klail City y sus alrededores* became *Klail City,* the *Claros varones de Belken* becomes *Fair Gentlemen of Belken County.* The other works, all in English, also reflect the changes undergone by both cultures up and down the two-thousand-mile Southwest border between the U.S. and Mexico. . . . The place and people are not only important, they are essential to me and to my writing.

Paul Horgan

The Southwest is large enough to include the widest varieties of terrain, and thus of weather and of human pursuits. It is a country of one of two characters: either there are immense plains, flat alike to the tempests and the endless days of sunlight, or there are mountains that challenge the zenith with the power of a legend. Only in the littlest local sense are there pastoral regions, with bounding green hills and sustained valleys. This meant that, looking for natural securities and havens, the early people found none; and the resultant exercise of human ingenuity and faith produced that crew of pioneers whose philosophy so often seemed almost geological in its simplicity and its strength. . . .

But men put upon a new country at once bring about marvels too exciting for silence. So it is the combination of land and people that gives history its earliest point of departure.

Dorothy B. Hughes

I know very well the seed of *Ride the Pink Horse*. It was at Fiesta in Santa Fe — with all the lights and music and colorful costumes — we all costumed Spanish and Mexican and Indian style in those days — and the gaiety. I thought: under the glitter there are problems, tragedy, even evil for some of the people. From that beginning came the usual "What if...," the trigger of all stories.

As for *The Blackbirder,* I had a book to write. My interest was always in suspense, and suspense at that time meant foreign goings-on. As I was living in Santa Fe at the time, I used that background. You can't research a New York or California book when you're in New Mexico.

Arturo Islas

I love the desert more than the sea. It is home to me despite its vastness and desolation. It is also a spiritual metaphor for my work, which includes mostly desert people. I like thinking that the desert — in all its glorious light — was once the bottom of the sea.

Writing is like going out into the desert by yourself.

Elmer Kelton

From almost any point on the Upton County ranch where I lived as a boy, I could see historic Castle Gap just to the southwest. My youthful imagination was fired by stories about events which happened there and at Horsehead Crossing just beyond. I listened in awe to old men who were living witnesses to some of that history. I was impressed very early by the toughness of the land and the toughness it imbues in the people who lived on it. It seemed to me, even then, that there was a uniqueness to the Southwest that should be perserved in story form, and I have been trying ever since to do so.

David Lavender

In my writing I am primarily concerned with following the twists and turns that the Western land has given to human ecological history. The West — all that naked rock, all that golden sunshine: how clear and aboveboard everything looks. But unexpected canyons slit the flatness; mountains rise unexpectedly out of tawny plains — hence the cliche', islands in the sky. Tensions are a fundamental part of the scenery. The long lines of mesas end in abrupt headlands, often marked, at the brink, by a last defiant finger or two that declines to topple when it should topple. Balances are precarious; bizarre forms commonplace. The arid West, we say, but the element that has shaped it beyond all others is water.

In this overly dry, scantily vegetated country, resources are few, easy to spot, and, as many developers have been deluded into thinking, ripe for the plucking. Unfortunately for these bold dreamers as they like to call themselves, there aren't enough goodies to go around. Or they prove stubborn. And so man's relationship with the land becomes man's relationship with his fellow invaders of the land. Sometimes the struggles are cooperative (the Mormon stake; the Telluride Chamber of Commerce); more often they are adversarial (the Shoot-out at the O.K. Corral or the greatest conflict of all where nary a pistol has yet popped, the tug-of-war over the Colorado River).

Recreationists, preservationists, exploiters, visionaries, all awash in the golden light. But they learn, they learn, just as the native dwellers have learned to adapt, to camouflage, to strike unexpectedly from places of concealment where there seems to be no concealment.

Tom Lea

I think D.H. Lawrence answers the question eloquently perhaps for all of us: "Every people is polarized in some particular locality, some home or homeland. And every great era of civilization seems to be the expression of a particular continent or continent region, as well as of the people concerned. There is, no doubt, some peculiar potentiality attaching to every distinct region of the earth's surface, over and above the indisputable facts of climate and geological condition. There is some subtle magnetic influence inherent in every specific locality, and it is this influence which keeps the inhabitant stable."

Harold Littlebird

I am a Native American of pueblo ancestry from Santo Domingo and Laguna Pueblos in New Mexico. I returned to New Mexico as a teenager, having lived in California and Utah most of my childhood.

About this time in my life, I was introduced to village ceremony as a participant in various ways. I began, first out of curiosity, to want to know more about my ancestry through religious practice. Then out of desire and ultimately, responsibility, I began to want to listen.

Through repeated ceremonial participation and involvement over the years, I have begun to be aware of limitless ancestral stories about this abundant Creation, passed on to generations through ritual guidance of song, practice, and prayer. I have been repeatedly told and shown how we, as human beings, are only one of many vital parts within creation and in our everyday lives there is the human task of understanding the interconnectedness of all life.

The value within the stories became focused and real as I began to observe in a different way the "writings" within my pueblo landscape. Geographic sites of ancient rock drawings and petroglyphs, along with religious shrines and numerous abandoned ruins, the ancestral homes of my forefathers, added meaning and visual definition to that tribal history I was just beginning to sense.

Having very little understanding of my native tongue, I use the English language as a tool for conveying my own creative expression, but that creativity has a greater source than just my cultural traditions. It becomes increasingly clear to me as I actively write poetry, compose contemporary songs, and joyfully celebrate daily life that the physical and spiritual landscape of my homeland, the Southwest, helps me obtain creativity. For this gift from the Creator, I am truly thankful.

Mark Medoff

Though born in the Midwest and raised in Miami Beach, Florida (a suburb of New York City), I grew up in Las Cruces and I am a New Mexican. The land and the people of the Southwest provide me inspiration as a writer and a peaceful and civilized place to live my other life as husband, father, and teacher.

Leon C. Metz

The Southwestern landscape played a role in my writing because, as fate would have it, I wound up living in West Texas. Back in 1963 I started writing book reviews for the El Paso *Times* and was assigned to Southwestern books. Gradually, I came to see that perhaps a book should be written on the different gunmen who lived in El Paso. I never set out to become a spokesman for Southwestern history. All I wanted to do was write a book, and I selected gunfighters because of their dramatic appeal.

At this point, I am too enchanted with the Southwest ever to write on other subjects. The Southwest (including northern Mexico) has the greatest, most untapped history in the United States. The Southwest will always be the hub of my writing.

N. Scott Momaday

Someone once said, "the writer is the intelligence of his soil." It is a true statement, and it seems to me the ultimate definition of a writer, any writer. In a sense, one's place, and his experience of it, is the only thing the writer has to write about. It is preeminently his subject. Certainly this is so in my case. With few exceptions, my writings have centered upon the Southwest. I can't think of a better geography upon which to center my writing, and I have seen much of the world. Finally, I suppose, we have no choice in the matter. We write of our time and place, and of our investment in that time and that place. Thank God. That's the way it ought to be. If I could choose any landscape in the world to write about, and to nourish my writing, it would be that of the American Southwest. Well, Soviet Central Asia (the foothills of the Pamirs) and northwest Greenland (Thule, Siorpaluk) are also endlessly wonderful to the mind. But the Southwest, the Southwest is mine.

Pat Mora

I am compelled to write by the pleasure I find in words and by my determination to preserve the Mexican American experience in English, the language I know best. The desert, *mi madre,* is my stern teacher. She is not a force compelling me to write; she is a subject or topic that has chosen me. The Southwestern landscape has been my world, my point of reference. If my poems succeed at any level, they should convey my feeling about *mi tierra*.

Gary Paul Nabhan

I don't believe in landscapes, but in living communities. The difference is that between backdrops and live actors. The plants, animals, and persistent cultures challenge me daily, not only to write, but to dream, and behave as if we should all try to make a contribution if we are to live here.

I don't see one Southwest, but many microhabitats, too diverse to be stereotyped as regional. A ground squirrel burrow, one canyon, a single saguaro, a particular Hispanic barrio, may be all the subject matter one needs.

John Nichols

The breadth, scope, and wildness of Southwestern terrain I suppose has always inspired me to want to transpose in words a landscape that is, in the vernacular, "larger than life." Not just the physical landscape but the human, the cultural, the historical landscape as well. Landscape here presupposes a human landscape, a social landscape, whose scope is heroic, and capable of transmitting a macroscopic overview of the world in all its magnificent convolutions. Weather, wildlife, sensational landscape, and the courage and mystery of human history in the Southwest has always triggered in me a desire to "rise to the occasion," as it were, and struggle to elucidate the dignity and adventure in all human endeavors, everywhere.

The balance of forces within the Southwestern landscape has always seemed to open up the metaphors of existence around the globe to excite me into wanting to join battle with all the struggles of human experience. Sounds corny, but landscape can be the triggering factor that unleashes such motivations. Nowhere else on earth have I seen the possibilities for things to proceed in such beauty towards hope for a positive future. Southwestern landscape, the parts of it that remain unbowed or undisturbed, seem to offer the deepest and most positive connections to our origins, and to a future where all is not destroyed.

Stanley Noyes

   A person writes out of his experience and imagination. If landscape is important to him, it will show in his work, can in fact be part of the impetus for that work. Space and silence under huge, changing skies are certainly congenial to the imagination. But so are cultural differences and tensions. So are strata of historical depths. Maybe a right conjunction of these elements can create the combustion which is a poem, a story, a novel.

   As for me, I have been and am intimately involved with New Mexico landscape. Winters I ski in the Sangre de Cristos. The rest of the year I hike in them weekly, as well as in the Sandias and the Jemez. Throughout the last thirteen years, when I worked for the New Mexico Arts Division, I've driven all over New Mexico. I love its skies above pink earth, its barrancas, its pinon and juniper hills, its plains, silky in the wind, its diverse cultures and historical dimensions. I know I draw a strength from it which helps me write. I know my writing, like a pond in Bosque del Apache, partially mirrors its landscape.

Lawrence Clark Powell

Landscape and literature. These are the two things that have come to have the strongest pull on me. Not history, not biography, or memoirs, or travel, or bibliography. No. The two l's, landscape and literature. Books that combine the beauty of the land with the beauty of the language. Books in which the thing described and the language of description are in perfect register, one overlying the other, so that there is no blur. Books in which the transparent language of literature affords the reader a clear look at landscape and life.

Jim Sagel

Just as the Southwestern landscape haunted me into forgetting about my return journey to what had once been my home, so too has this austere and rugged *paisaje* compelled me to write. Like a lover always coaxing me to the brink of satisfaction, this landscape of chiseled red mesas and aging mountains endlessly fascinates me, never leaving my writing alone, always dancing into the picture.

A sense of "place," I think is vital to any good writing, but nowhere more than in the Southwest is "place" so integrally wrapped up in the daily details of living. I can't conceive of my characters without painting in their environment which has done so much to shape them, from their ancestors down through the centuries. Doña Agueda is not Doña Agueda without the muddy waters of the *acequia* lazily meandering through her rows of chile plants ripening under a blazing sky. Nor can I imagine Uncle Steven without seeing the Pueblo elder cutting red river reeds at the confluence of the Rio Chama and the Rio Grande where his distant ancestors once received those strange armored and bewhiskered colonizers from another world. One, of course, might be able to overstate the importance of the landscape, but I'm not sure how. Even the lowriders cruising into chrome-plated infinity can't be isolated from the Lotaburgers landmarking their relentless journey.

It is not solely the fact that this land and impossible sky are, as Simón Ortiz once said, like a pretty woman looking back at us. The essential point is that this landscape has not only inspired me, but has also shaped the characters that inhabit my writings. For me, the landscape and the people that dwell in it are one, just as the fictional universe I create overlaps and resonates with the real world I live in along this great and ancient river.

Ricardo Sánchez

Amongst all the definitions which I use to make sense of my human existence, i.e., human being, man, Chicano, etc., another is of equal import: *hombre nacido y curtido por lo indefinible del desierto.* Born to umbrage of a desert sun, molded by the expanse of land — frontiers which do not exist as other than ideas for the horizon is beyond visibility — I revel and celebrate the immensity of the desert, its continuity and permanence, and those images are important to me.

Nurtured by El Paso's rich array of diverse imagery, I feel sutured by the transformation of desert into an oasis created by hardy dreamers. There is a solace, a serenity, and an overwhelming majesty about the desert. Rugged, the land demands commitment from its peoples. Survival is a harsh confrontation with the elements, but it is not a cynical, uncaring cycle of cruelties. It is a strengthening test, one which forces one to explore the delicate balances between fragile skeins of life and the rigidity of arbitrary death....

The Southwest has been the natal home of my family — both patrilineal and matrilineal — since before there were any English-speaking colonies on the Eastern Seaboard, thus I feel that I am the rivers, mountains, deserts and valleys/plateaus of my land. It is "la madre tierra," and I celebrate it in its beauty, majesty, power, serenity, and/or violence.

Jack Schaefer

The Southwest landscape never compelled me to write anything. I was an established writer long before I got into the Southwest. It has had some effect on what I have written since, but I would have kept on writing whether or not I ever came near the Southwest. I probably wouldn't have written in the same way. I'm sure I wouldn't have written *Old Ramon,* for example, not having been out here. Those stories like *Monte Walsh,* which I did over a series of ten or twelve years, would have been different, and I probably wouldn't have placed them in the Southwest, in New Mexico, but probably in Wyoming or Montana. The Southwest has had a lot of influence on my writing, but it certainly hasn't compelled me to do anything.

Marc Simmons

I find the Southwest, particularly New Mexico, a place where past and present meet — cojoin — to produce an atmosphere highly conducive to the creative process. Here, history *counts* and those who deal with historical themes find themselves much in demand. Some of the best regional writing in America, I believe, is coming and has come from the Southwest. Perhaps it is because the stark landscape and the rich cultural heritage impose themselves as much upon writers as they do upon artists.

John L. Sinclair

I'll tell you what the Southwestern landscape is: the sky, the mesa, the mountains, the sagebrush, the greasewood, the sand, the gravel, the horned toads, the rattlesnakes. God, I love them and I love the people who live way out in the desert like I do. I'm a recluse. Gosh, I don't go anywhere. Why do I write about the people in the desert? Because I know them. I've got them here in my guts. They are the people I knew back sixty-three years ago. I would not have written had I not lived in the Southwest.

Joseph Somoza

My early poems were written from a Midwestern perspective, with Midwestern images and a Midwestern density. After living in New Mexico for a few years, my poems got sparser, with bigger spaces between the lines and stanzas and between the title and the poem. Today I prefer stark, uncluttered poems. The physical traits that I like best about the Southwest are the thin air and the uncluttered landscape — both of which enable me to see for a long way.

C. L. Sonnichsen

Nothing compelled me to write (I do not think of myself as an artist, or even a writer). I chose to write. As a Midwestern product educated in the East, I found Texas a strange and wonderful place and I wanted to know more about it, but it was the people rather than the landscape which got me excited and made me eager to record what I saw and learned. Of course the people were the product of the land and I was eager to explore their relationship with their environment, but the people were paramount — their faces, their history, their folkways. The fact that I was a feud specialist and spent a good many years pursuing my interest shows what impelled me to write. My basic preoccupation at all times was the literature of the Southwest, particularly the Southwestern novel, and since the land itself is almost always a major ingredient in our regional fiction, I got back to the landscape, indirectly, in that way.

Stan Steiner

The mountains, the land, the sun, the sky are the subject of everything I write.
It's that simple/

Elizabeth Tallent

When I was five I had a fantasy of finding a place where, however faraway the horizon line was, there would be nothing man-made in what I could see. My father was a research biochemist then, as young as I am now, and for work or his own pleasure — I've never been sure which — he would drive us children out on Saturdays to fields he knew, where some experimental hybrid of corn or soy was being nursed, in an acre-square, sweet green plane of shoots or paired leaves, up from black, black Illinois earth. I never had to look far to find the thing, telephone line or distant shed, that marred the emptiness for me, and once I'd found it, I lost interest, and began to torment my sister; or she and I would gang up on our younger brother. My father's pleasure in such fields was very keen. It troubled him that his children could never be silent for long, even in a place he considered ideal.

My five-year-old's game remained, half-forgotten, an undercurrent in my sense of what is beautiful, until in New Mexico I found a terrain that nothing, no flaw, could rule out, and my love for where I live is partly founded on the way in which what I was seeing undid my habit of seeing and discounting. "Beautiful" is one thing I think about certain fawn-walled desert canyons, but there are other, stronger responses, among them an unpredictable sense of my own all-rightness when I am there. It is a sense I find hard to pin down or analyze, though I suppose it is similar to what my father felt, facing a field of fluttering new-minted soy leaves, the exact match, chromosomally, of nothing that had ever grown on earth before. What I feel facing a scroll of desert varnish that has unreeled down a gold cliff, or snowmelt running in an arroyo bottom, is delight, and a deep wish that they should continue to be as they are, and that I could stand still for hours. And from this distance I know what my father felt, when to leave you have to tear yourself away.

Luci Tapahonso

The land is an integral part of my history, my life and even my name. As a Navajo person, I was taught that we emerged, originated out of the earth from other worlds that occurred before this one. This particular place is in Northwestern New Mexico in the Four Corners area. The deity and center of all life in the Navajo cosmos is "Naa asdzaa" — Mother Earth. My identity as a Navajo person is my mother's clan — "Too diizhooshii" — Bitter Water clan. My last name, Tapahonso, is the "Beside the Big Water" people. These are all ways of identifying myself and these elements are the person that I am — a mother, a daughter, teacher and one who writes. The landscape plays an important role in my writing because it is part of the Navajo consciousness and lifestyle.

Sabine R. Ulibarrí

There is a mystique and a magic, a majesty and a miracle in the air of the skyscapes and the landscapes of the lands of New Mexico. The skies are high and blue. The horizons are distant and blue. The light is bright. The air is clear. The play of light and shadow on the land hypnotizes. The interplay of line and color mesmerizes. The smells of the high sierras and the lowland deserts intoxicate. The whispering sounds of streams and pines rock and lull. The vastness, the stillness, and the silence overwhelm you.

Such is Nuevo México. Overpowering. Nature in the nude in all its beauty, violence, and strength. Stark, physical, and sensual. With infinite, unfathomable spiritual dimensions. There it is: a challenge, a threat, a hope, and a promise. Those of us who live here gaze upon this timeless, limitless place in awe and silent reverence, imbued with a love that has no equal.

The land and the sky demand a response. There is a story to be told, a song to be sung, a picture to be painted, a rug to be woven, a santo to be carved. We all do, each in our own way. We who write, sing, paint, weave or carve are part of the greatscape. We are the voice of Nuevo México.

So the land, the river, and the sky flow into my soul and through my arm unto my writings.

Frank Waters

The belief that the global earth is a living organism has been held since ancient times by the great civilizations of the Middle and Far East, and by all Indian America from Central America to our own contemporary Southwest.

I adhere to this belief myself, rather than to the dominating Anglo-American premise that the earth is inanimate matter, mere real estate, to be exploited at will.

Certainly every continent, country, and region has its own distinctive spirit of place, its own rhythm, which it imparts to its species of animals, plants, and human races. The drumbeat of native Africa is different from that of Indian America, although both echo the pulse of one common life force.

The vibratory quality of even a neighborhood or barrio in a large city, apart from its cultural milieu, can be sensed immediately. It exudes a feeling of peace or hostility without apparent cause, just as we feel attraction or repulsion to a person we meet for the first time.

Places have always affected me like this. Not only the Southwest as an area which seems to imbue the strongest creative life force, but the various localities which have drawn and held me. All of my books, in some way, are about these places and about persons who have been affected by their distinctive influences.

Marta Weigle

I have always felt that the Southwest allows people to fill the space they should properly occupy — not inflate beyond it or cower beneath it. With that freedom also comes clarity and subtlety. Light, wind, and clouds take the place of the sea. The fascination comes too from movement through the immensity — by foot, horseback, train, or automobile. Some of this movement is mythic, and I sense it as a journey of emergence up through worlds. Some of it is migratory like the pilgrimage to Chimayo or the Way of the Cross. Horses, carts, trains, and cars also have their peculiar symbolic qualities in human journeying through sacred inner and outer space in this land. I am now trying to capture the meanings of that movement to, across, and through immensity from the mythic and heroic migrations and journeys to the secular pilgrimage of tourists in both fiction and nonfiction writings.

Jeanne Williams

The Rio Grande Valley of Texas introduced me to a main theme: the clashing cultures along the border and again the human saga in the brazada. For thirty years now, the Southwest has inspired most of my work. Since moving to Arizona, I have camped and travelled often along the Sea of Cortez and in the Pinacate region of Mexico. That weirdly beautiful region of cinder cones, lava flows, and dunes is perhaps my favorite Other Land though for living I love where I am — right in the mouth of Cave Creek Canyon in the Chiricahuas. I often hike in them and in the Peloncillos just over the New Mexico line. The country with its plains yielding to mountains that have springs and trees hidden back inside is endlessly fascinating. Only desert dwellers can fully appreciate running water and shade.

Loving the wilds, I am concerned about their being destroyed and this is also a strong thread in my work. I admire the creatures from lizards to hawks that make a living here and salute them as my neighbors. Also, the succor hidden in spiny plants and the way Native Americans survived here intrigues me. Many campsites are in this area. I like to sit by the grinding holes and imagine women working and chatting while the children play. I have lived in various parts of the Southwest and might move around in it, but I would never live anywhere else.

Keith Wilson

I was born here — grew up bilingual and have always been in love with the desert, its peoples, both two-legged and otherwise. The land has its voice and I am happiest when I can hear its tones in my poems.

Norman Zollinger

In my fiction my strong feeling for the land has almost made it an added "character." It doesn't surprise me, for instance, that almost all of mankind's great religions have evolved in desert and wilderness regions. Man is so strongly influenced by terrain it is no wonder that people who tell stories are, as well.

Ann Zwinger

I was compelled to write by an interest in natural history that began in the mountains of Colorado. By chance I wrote about the Green River and was introduced to the Southwest.

I have never felt "compelled" to write by the Southwest landscape. I write about it because I am at home there and find it infinitely fascinating on many levels. Although I have written and do write about other parts of the country, I probably gravitate more to the desert than anything else and that includes more territory than what I understand the Southwest to be.

I consider that I write natural history first and am a regional writer second, and the region happens to be, largely, the Southwest. And the Southwest provides a kind of light and space and clarity that I do not find elsewhere.

LIVES & WORKS

Edward Abbey

Born: Home, Pennsylvania, 1927.
Education: University of New Mexico, 1947-1951. Edinburgh University, 1951-1952. Stanford University, 1957-1958.
Career: Worked for sixteen seasons as a seasonal ranger, fire fighter, and fire lookout for the National Park Service and the U.S. Forest Service.
Awards: Fulbright Fellow, 1951. Guggenheim Fellow, 1976.
Residence: Oracle, Arizona.

Selected Bibliography

Jonathan Troy. New York: Dodd, Mead and Company, 1954.
The Brave Cowboy. New York: Dodd, Mead and Company, 1956.
Fire on the Mountain. New York: Dial Press, 1962.
Desert Solitaire. New York: McGraw-Hill, 1968.
Appalachian Wilderness: The Great Smoky Mountains (with Eliot Porter). New York: Dutton, 1970.
Black Sun. New York: Simon and Schuster, 1971.
Slickrock: The Canyon Country of Southeast Utah (with Philip Hyde). New York: Sierra Club, 1971.
Cactus Country (with Ernest Haas). New York: Time-Life Books, 1973.
The Monkey Wrench Gang. Philadelphia: J.B. Lippincott, 1975.
The Journey Home. New York: E.P. Dutton, 1977.
The Hidden Canyon (with John Blaustein). New York: Viking Press, 1977.
Desert Images (with David Muench). New York: Chanticleer Press, 1979.
Abbey's Road. New York: E.P. Dutton, 1979.
Good News. New York: E.P. Dutton, 1980.
Down the River. New York: E.P. Dutton, 1982.
Beyond the Wall. New York: Holt, Rinehart, 1984.
Slumgullion Stew: A Reader. New York: E.P. Dutton, 1985.
One Life At A Time, Please. New York: Holt and Company, 1987.
The Fool's Progress. New York: Holt and Company, 1988.

Lee K. Abbott

Born: Panama Canal Zone, 17 October 1947.
Education: New Mexico State University, B.A., 1970; M.A., 1973. University of Arkansas, M.F.A., 1977.
Career: Case Western Reserve University, professor of English, 1977-present.
Awards: National Endowment for the Arts Fellowship, 1979, 1985. St. Lawrence Award for Fiction, 1981. Cleveland Arts Prize, 1982. Ohio Arts Prize, 1982. Best American Short Stories, 1984, 1987. O. Henry Prize, 1984. Story Quarterly Prize for Fiction, 1985. National Magazine Award for Fiction, 1986. Editor's Choice Prize, 1986. Pushcart Prize, 1986.
Residence: University Heights, Ohio.

Selected Bibliography

The Heart Never Fits Its Wanting. Cedar Falls, Iowa: North American Review, 1980.
Love Is The Crooked Thing. Chapel Hill, N.C.: Algonquin Books of Chapel Hill, 1986.
Strangers in Paradise. New York: G.P. Putnam's Sons, 1987.

Rudolfo A. Anaya

Born: Pastura, New Mexico, 30 October 1937.
Education: University of New Mexico, B.A., Literature, 1963. University of New Mexico, M.A., Literature, 1968.
Career: University of New Mexico, Department of English, associate professor, 1974-1987; professor, 1987-present.
Awards: Premio Quinto Sol, national literary award for *Bless Me, Ultima*. National Endowment for the Arts Creative Writing Fellowship, 1979. New Mexico Governor's Award for excellence and achievement in literature, 1980. Honorary degrees from University of Albuquerque and Marycrest College, Davenport, Iowa.
Residence: Albuquerque, New Mexico.

Selected Bibliography

Bless Me, Ultima. Berkeley: Tonatiuh International, 1972.
Heart of Aztlán. Berkeley: Editorial Justa Publications, 1976.
Tortuga. Berkeley: Editorial Justa Publications, 1979.
Cuentos: Tales From the Hispanic Southwest. Santa Fe: Museum of New Mexico Press, 1980.
Ceremony of Brotherhood (coeditor). Albuquerque: Academia Publications, 1980.
The Silence of the Llano. Berkeley: Tonatiuh-Quinto Sol, 1982.
The Legend of Llorona. Berkeley: Tonatiuh-Quinto Sol, 1982.
Cuentos Chicanos: A Short Story Anthology (coeditor). Albuquerque: University of New Mexico Press, 1984.
The Adventures of Juan Chicaspatas. Houston: Arte Público Press, 1985.
A Chicano in China. Albuquerque: University of New Mexico Press, 1986.
Voces: An Anthology of Nuevo Mexicano Writers (editor). Albuquerque: El Norte Publications, 1987.
Lord of the Dawn - The Legend of Quetzalcoatl. Albuquerque: University of New Mexico Press, 1987.
The Farolitos of Christmas. Santa Fe: New Mexico Magazine, 1987.

Byrd Baylor

Born: San Antonio, Texas, 28 March 1924.
Awards: Caldecott Honor Book Awards for *The Desert is Theirs, Hawk I'm Your Brother, The Way to Start A Day*, and *When Clay Sings*. Catlin Peace Pipe Award from the American Indian Lore Society. Named outstanding Arizona author by the Arizona Library Association, 1985.
Residence: Arivaca, Arizona.

Selected Bibliography

Amigo. New York: Macmillan, 1963.
One Small Blue Bead. New York: Macmillan, 1965.
Before You Came This Way. New York: E.P. Dutton, 1969.
When Clay Sings. New York: Scribner's, 1972.
Coyote Cry. New York: Lothrop, 1972.
Sometimes I Dance Mountains. New York: Scribner's, 1973.
Everybody Needs A Rock. New York: Scribner's, 1974.
They Put On Masks. New York: Scribner's, 1974.
The Desert Is Theirs. New York: Scribner's, 1975.
We Walk In Sandy Places. New York: Scribner's, 1976.
Hawk, I'm Your Brother. New York: Scribner's, 1976.

And It Is Still That Way. New York: Scribner's, 1976.
Guess Who My Favorite Person Is. New York: Scribner's, 1977.
Yes Is Better Than No. New York: Scribner's, 1977.
The Other Way To Listen. New York: Scribner's, 1978.
The Way To Start A Day. New York: Scribner's, 1978.
Your Own Best Secret Place. New York: Scribner's, 1979.
If You Are A Hunter Of Fossils. New York: Scribner's, 1980.
A God On Every Mountain Top. New York: Scribner's, 1981.
Desert Voices. New York: Scribner's, 1981.
Moon Song. New York: Scribner's, 1982.
The Best Town In The World. New York: Scribner's, 1982.
I'm In Charge Of Celebrations. New York: Scribner's, 1986.

Elroy Bode

Born: Kerrville, Texas, 2 August 1931.
Education: University of Texas at Austin, B.A., English; B.S., Education, summa cum laude, Phi Beta Kappa, 1954.
Career: Teacher, Texas public schools of Sinton, 1954-1955; Kerrville, 1957-1958; El Paso, 1958-1959, 1961-1982; and Garland, 1959-1961; Bandera Junior High, Bandera, Texas, 1982-1984; John Jay High School, San Antonio, 1984-1986; Austin High School, El Paso, 1986-present.
Awards: El Paso Independent School District Teacher of the Year, 1977-1978. Border Regional Library Association Award, C.L. Sonnichsen Publication Award, *To Be Alive,* 1979. El Paso Herald-Post Writers Hall of Fame, Inductee, 1986.
Residence: El Paso, Texas.

Selected Bibliography

Texas Sketchbook. El Paso: Texas Western Press, 1967.
Sketchbook II. El Paso: Texas Western Press, 1972.
Alone: In the World: Looking. El Paso: Texas Western Press, 1973.
Home and Other Moments. El Paso: Texas Western Press, 1975.
To Be Alive. El Paso: Texas Western Press, 1979.
This Favored Place. Fredericksburg: Shearer Publishing Company, 1983.

Richard Bradford

Born: Chicago, Illinois, 1 May 1932.
Education: Tulane University, B.A., 1952.
Residence: Santa Fe, New Mexico.

Selected Bibliography

Red Sky at Morning. New York: J.B. Lippincott, 1968.
So Far From Heaven. New York: J.B. Lippincott, 1973.

Ernest J. Burrus, S.J.

Born: El Paso, Texas, 20 April 1907.
Education: Gonzaga University, Spokane, Washington, A.B., M.A., Philosophy, 1932. Loyola University, M.A., Latin and Greek Classics, 1933-1934. Studied theology at Ignatiuskolleg at Valkenburg, Holland and at Imperial Austrian University of Innsbruck. Attended Mont Laurier in Canada; Catholic University, Washington, D.C. and Laval University, Quebec, Canada.
Career: Entered the Jesuit Order at St. Charles College, Loyola University, 1925. Instructor, Loyola University, 1932-1935, 1939-1950. Staff member, Jesuit Historical Institute, Rome, Italy, 1950-present. Research professor, University of Arizona, 1975-1978. Assistant pastor, Sacred Heart Church, El Paso, Texas, 1978-present.
Awards: Fellowship in Carnegie Grant in Aid Program, 1946-1951. Guggenheim Fellowships, 1957-1959. St. Louis University, LL.D., 1960. American Council of Learned Societies, 1966. Philosophical Society, 1967. Chosen one of the eminent historians for 1985 by the *Hispanic American Historical Review*. Loyola University, Doctor of Humane Letters, 1987.
Residence: El Paso, Texas.

Selected Bibliography

Kino Reports to Headquarters. Rome: Institutum Historicum Societatis Jesu, 1954.
Editor with Felix Zubillaga, S.J., Francisco Javier Alegre, S.J., *Historia de la Compañía de Jesús en Nueva España*. Rome: Institutum Historicum Societatis Jesu, 1956-1960.
Editor: *Correspondencia del P. Kino con los Generales de la Compañía de Jesús, 1682-1707*. Mexico City: Editorial Jus, 1961.
Editor of Eusebio F. Kino, S.J., *Vida del P. Francisco J. Saeta, S.J.: Sangre misionera en Sonora*. Mexico City: Editorial Jus, 1961.
Editor: *Kino's Plan for the Development of Pimería Alta, Arizona and Upper California. A Report to the Mexican Viceroy*. Tucson: Arizona Pioneers' Historical Society, 1961.
Editor of Francisco María Piccolo, S.J., *Informe del estado de la nueva cristiandad de California, 1702, y otros documentos*. Madrid: José Porrúa Turanzas, 1692.
Editor: *Kino escribe a la Duquesa. Correspondencia del P. Eusebio F. Kino con la Duquesa de Aveiro y otros documentos*. Madrid: José Porrua Turanzas, 1964.
Kino Writes to the Duchess. Letters and Reports of the Missonary Explorer to the Duchess of Aveiro in Spain, 1680-1687. Rome: Institutum Historicum Societatis Jesu, 1965.
Kino and the Cartography of Northwestern New Spain. Tucson: Arizona Pioneers' Historical Society, 1965.
La obra cartográfica de la provincia mexicana de la Compañía de Jesús, 1567-1967, 2 vol. Madrid: José Porrúa Turanzas, 1967.
Editor of Fernando de Rivera y Moncada, *Diario del capitán Fernando de Rivera y Moncada*, 2 vols. Madrid: José Porrúa Turanzas, 1967.
Translator and editor: *The Writings of Alonso de la Vera Cruz*, 5 vols. Rome: Institutum Historicum Societatis Jesu, 1968-1976.
Author and editor of Adolph F. Bandelier, *A History of the Southwest, Vol. I. A Catalogue of the Bandelier Collection in the Vatican Library; With a Supplement to Vol. I: Reproduction in Color of Thirty Sketches and of Ten Maps*. Rome: Institutum Historicum Societatis Jesu and the Vatican Library, 1969. The three volumes of text are in preparation.

Kino and Manje, Explorers of Sonora and Arizona: Their Vision of the Future. A Study of the Expeditions and Plans, with an Appendix of Thirty Documents. Map of the Area and Place Finder by Ronald I. Ives. Rome: Institutum Historicum Societatis Jesu, 1971.
Translator and editor of Juan María de Salvatierra, S.J., *Selected Letters About Lower California.* Los Angeles: Dawson's Book Shop, 1971.
Editor with Felix Zubillaga, S.J., *Misiones Mexicanas de la Compañía de Jesus, 1618-1745: Cartas e informes conservados en la "Coleccion Mateu."* Madrid: José Porrúa Turanzas, 1982.
Translator and editor: *Jesuit Relations: Baja California, 1716-1762.* Los Angeles: Dawson's Book Shop, 1984.
Author with Gloria Grajales, *Bibliografía Guadalupana (1531-1984): Guadalupan Bibliography (1531-1984).* Washington, D.C.: Georgetown University Press, 1986.
Editor with Felix Zubillaga, *Documentos sobre las Misiones Norteñas de los Jesuitas Mexicanos, 1601-1762.* Mexico City: University of Mexico, 1987.

Fray Angélico Chávez

Born: Wagon Mound, New Mexico, 10 April 1910. Descended from Spanish families which settled New Mexico in 1598 and 1693.
Education: Franciscan seminaries and colleges in Cincinnati, Detroit, and Oldenburg, Indiana, 1924-1937.
Career: Ordained a Franciscan in Santa Fe, 6 May 1937. Served Franciscan Missions in New Mexico, 1937-1972. Army chaplain, 1943-1946. Made beachhead landings on Guam and Leyte with 77th Infantry Division. Served in Germany with occupation troops, 1951-1952. Retired from ministerial work, 1972, but still helping archbishop of Santa Fe with church archives and restoration of his cathedral.
Awards: University of New Mexico, honorary M.A. and Ph.D. University of Albuquerque and New Mexico State University, honorary LL.D. Catholic Poetry Society, New York, Medallion. Conference of Christians and Jews Award. Historical Society of New Mexico Award, 1987. New Mexico Endowment for the Humanities, 1987.
Residence: Santa Fe, New Mexico.

Selected Bibliography
Clothed With The Sun. Santa Fe: Writers' Editions, 1939.
New Mexico Triptych. Paterson, N.J.: St. Anthony Guild Press, 1940.
Seraphic Days. Paterson, N.J.: St. Anthony Guild Press, 1940.
Eleven Lady-Lyrics. Paterson, N.J.: St. Anthony Guild Press, 1945.
The Single Rose. Santa Fe: Los Santos Bookshop, 1948.
Our Lady of the Conquest. Santa Fe: Historical Society of New Mexico, 1948.
La Conquistadora. Paterson, N.J.: St. Anthony Guild Press, 1954.
Origins of New Mexico Families. Santa Fe: Historical Society of New Mexico, 1954.
Missions of New Mexico (with E.B. Adams). Albuquerque: University of New Mexico Press, 1956.
Archives of the Archdiocese of Santa Fe. Washington, D.C.: Academy of American Franciscan History, 1957.
From An Altar Screen. New York: Farrar Straus, 1957.
The Virgin of Port Lligat. Fresno: Academy Guild Press, 1959.
The Lady from Toledo. Fresno: Academy Guild Press, 1960.

Coronado's Friars. Washington, D.C.: Academy of American Franciscan History, 1968.
Selected Poems. Santa Fe: Press of the Territorian, 1969.
The Oroz Codex. Washington, D.C.: Academy of American Franciscan History, 1972.
The Song of Francis. Flagstaff: Northland Press, 1974.
My Penitente Land. Albuquerque: University of New Mexico Press, 1974.
The Domínguez-Escalante Journal. Provo: Brigham Young University Press, 1976.
But Time and Chance. Santa Fe: Sunstone Press, 1981.
Tres Macho — He Said. Santa Fe: Gannon Publisher, 1985.
The Short Stories of Fray Angélico Chávez (edited by Genaro M. Padilla). Albuquerque: University of New Mexico Press, 1988.

Denise Chávez

Born: Las Cruces, New Mexico, 15 August 1948.
Education: New Mexico State University, B.A., Theatre, 1971. Trinity University, San Antonio, Texas, M.F.A., Theatre, 1974. University of New Mexico, M.A., Creative Writing, 1984.
Career: Northern New Mexico Community College, taught English Composition and Literature, 1975-1977. State of New Mexico, Artist-in-the-Schools Program, 1980-present.
Awards: New Mexico State University Literary Award for playwriting, 1970. National Endowment for the Arts and New Mexico Arts Division, Writers in Residency Fellowship, 1981. University of New Mexico, Writing Fellowship, 1982. National Endowment for the Arts, Inter-Arts Grant for *Hecho en Mexico*, 1982. Rockefeller Playwriting Fellowship, 1985. New Mexico Arts Division Grants for works in progress, 1986.
Residence: Las Cruces, New Mexico.

Selected Bibliography
The Last of the Menu Girls. Houston: Arte Publico Press, 1986.

Plays
Novitiates. 1971.
Elevators. 1972.
Mario and the Room María. 1974.
The Flying Tortilla Man. 1975.
Rainy Day Waterloo. 1976.
The Mask of November. 1976.
The Third Door. 1978.
Nacimiento. 1979.
The Adobe Rabbit. 1979.
Santa Fe Charm. 1980.
Si, Hay Posada. 1980.
Cruz Blanca, Story of A Town. 1981.
El Santero de Cordóva. 1981.
Hecho en México (with Nita Luna). 1982.
The Green Madonna. 1982.
La Morenita. 1983.
Francis! 1983.
El Más Pequeño de Mis Hijos. 1983.
Plague-Time. 1984.
Plaza. 1984.
Novena Narrativas. 1986.
Language of Vision. 1987.

Peggy Pond Church

Born: Near Watrous, Mora County, New Mexico, 1 December 1903.
Died: Santa Fe, New Mexico, 24 October 1986.
Education: Smith College, B.A., 1926.
Awards: New Mexico Governor's Award for Excellence in the Arts, 1984.

Selected Bibliography

Foretaste. Santa Fe: Writer's Editions, 1933.
The Burro Of Angelitos. New York: Sutton House, 1936.
Familiar Journey. Santa Fe: Writer's Editions, 1936.
Ultimatum For Man. Stanford, Calif.: James Ladd Delkin, 1946.
The House At Otowi Bridge. Albuquerque: University of New Mexico Press, 1960.
New And Selected Poems. Boise, Idaho: Ahsahta Press, Boise State University, 1976.
The Ripened Fields. Santa Fe: Lightning Tree, 1978.
A Rustle Of Angels. Denver: Peartree Press, 1981.
Birds Of Daybreak. Santa Fe: William Gannon, 1985.

William Eastlake

Born: New York, New York, 14 July 1917.
Education: Attended Alliance Francaise, Paris, 1948-1950.
Career: Lecturer, University of New Mexico, 1967-1968; University of Southern California, 1968-1969; University of Arizona, 1969-1971; United States Military Academy, 1975. Knox College, Galesburg, Illinois, writer in residence, 1967.
Awards: Ford Foundation Grant, 1963. Rockefeller Foundation Grant, 1966, 1967. University of Albuquerque, LL.D., 1970. Les Lettres Nouvelles Award for best foreign novel published in France, 1972.
Residence: Bisbee, Arizona.

Selected Bibliography

Go In Beauty. New York: Harper and Brothers, 1956.
The Bronc People. New York: Harcourt, Brace and Company, 1958.
Portrait Of An Artist With 26 Horses. New York: Simon and Schuster, 1963.
Castle Keep. New York: Simon and Schuster, 1965.
The Bamboo Bed. New York: Simon and Schuster, 1969.
A Child's Garden Of Verses For The Revolution. New York: Grove Press, 1970.
Dancers In The Scalp House. New York: Viking Press, 1975.
The Long Naked Descent Into Boston. New York: Viking Press, 1977.
Jack Armstrong In Tangier. Flint, Mich.: Bamberger Books, 1984.

Max Evans

Born: Ropes, Texas, 29 August 1924.
Career: Working cowboy, rancher, miner, painter, documentary filmmaker, screenwriter.
Awards: Western Writers of America Golden Spur Award. Cowboy Hall of Fame Wrangler Award. City of Las Angeles Commendation Award. Honorary Life Member, University of Texas System Chancellor's Council.
Residence: Albuquerque, New Mexico.

Selected Bibliography

Southwest Wind. San Antonio: Naylor, 1958.
Long John Dunn Of Taos. Los Angeles: Westernlore Press, 1959.
The Rounders. New York: Macmillan, 1960.
The Hi Lo Country. New York: Macmillan, 1961.
One-Eyed Sky. Boston: Houghton Mifflin, 1962.
The Mountain Of Gold. Dunwoody, Ga.: Norman S. Berg, 1965.
Shadow Of Thunder. Chicago: Swallow Press, 1969.
My Pardner. Boston: Houghton Mifflin, 1972.
Sam Peckinpah: Master Of Violence. Vermillion, S. Dak.: Dakota Press, University of South Dakota, 1972.
Bobby Jack Smith, You Dirty Coward. Los Angeles: Nash Publishing, 1974.
The White Shadow. San Diego: Joyce Press, 1977.
The Great Wedding. Albuquerque: University of New Mexico Press, 1983.
Xavier's Folly And Other Stories. Albuquerque: University of New Mexico Press, 1984.
Super Bull. Albuquerque: University of New Mexico Press, 1986.

Floyd S. Fierman

Born: Cleveland, Ohio, 16 May 1916.
Education: John Carroll University, Cleveland, Ohio, Ph.B., 1939. Hebrew Union College, Cincinnati, Ohio, B.H.L., 1943; M.H.L., 1945. University of Pittsburgh, Ph.D., Department of Education, 1949.
Career: Rodef Shalom Congregation, Pittsburgh, rabbi, 1945-1949. Temple Mt. Sinai, El Paso, Texas, rabbi, 1949-1979; resident scholar, 1979-present. University of Texas at El Paso, visiting lecturer in Philosophy, 1958-1970.
Awards: Hebrew Union College, Cincinnati, Doctor of Divinity degree.
Residence: El Paso, Texas.

Selected Bibliography

Some Early Jewish Settlers On The Southwestern Frontier. El Paso: Texas Western Press, 1960.
Merchant Bankers Of Early Santa Fe, 1844-1893. El Paso: Texas Western Press, 1964.
Samuel Freudenthal, El Paso Merchant and Civic Leader. El Paso: Texas Western Press, 1965.
The Schwartz Family Of El Paso. El Paso: Texas Western Press, 1980.
Insights and Hindsights Of Some El Paso Jewish Families. El Paso: El Paso Jewish Historical Society, 1983.
Insights and Hindsights Of Some More El Paso Jewish Families. El Paso: El Paso Jewish Historical Society, 1984.

Guts and Ruts: The Jewish Pioneer On The Trail In the American Southwest. New York: KTAV Publishing House, 1985.

Roots and Boots: From Crypto-Jew In New Spain To Community Leader In The American Southwest. Hoboken, N.J.: KTAV Publishing House, 1987.

Bernard Fontana

Born: Oakland, California, 7 January 1931.

Education: University of California, Berkeley, B.A., Anthropology, 1953. University of Arizona, Ph.D., Anthropology, 1960.

Career: University of Arizona Library, field historian, 1960-1962, 1978-present. Arizona State Museum, ethnologist, 1962-1978. University of Arizona, lecturer in Anthropology, 1962-1978; special assistant to the president, 1978-1982.

Awards: University of California Alumni Scholar. University of Arizona Graduate Fellowship. Wenner-Gren Foundation for Anthropological Research Pre-doctoral Fellowship. Border Regional Library Association Awards for *Tarahumara*, 1979, and *Of Earth and Little Rain,* 1981. Arizona-Nevada Academy of Science, Elected Fellow, 1985.

Residence: Tucson, Arizona.

Selected Bibliography

Johnny Ward's Ranch (with Cameron Greenleaf and others). Tucson: Arizona Archaeological and Historical Society, 1962.

Papago Indian Pottery (with William J. Robinson and others). Seattle: University of Washington Press, 1962.

Mission San Xavier Del Bac (with photographs by Helga Teiwes). Tucson: University of Arizona Press, 1973.

The Papago Tribe of Arizona. New York and London: Garland Publishing Company, 1974.

Indians Of Arizona: A Contemporary Perspective (with Thomas Weaver and others). Tucson: University of Arizona Press, 1974.

Friar Bringas Reports To The King: Methods Of Indoctrination On The Frontier Of New Spain (edited, with Daniel S. Matson). Tucson: University of Arizona Press, 1976.

The Other Southwest: Indian Arts And Crafts Of Northwestern Mexico (with Edmond J.B. Faubert and Barney T. Burns). Phoenix: Heard Museum, 1977.

Tarahumara: Where Night Is The Day Of The Moon (with photographs by John P. Schaefer). Flagstaff: Northland Press, 1979.

The Material World Of The Tarahumara. Tucson: Arizona State Museum, 1979.

Of Earth And Little Rain: The Papago Indians (with photographs by John P. Schaefer). Flagstaff: Northland Press, 1979.

Massacre On The Gila (with Clifton B. Kroeber). Tucson: University of Arizona Press, 1986.

Chickens. Tumacacori, Ariz.: Tumacacori Press, 1987.

Gene Frumkin

Born: New York, 29 January 1928.
Education: University of California at Los Angeles, B.A., English, 1951.
Career: *California Apparel News,* managing editor and executive editor, 1952-1966. University of New Mexico, lecturer, assistant professor, associate professor of English, 1966-present.
Residence: Albuquerque, New Mexico.

Selected Bibliography

The Hawk And The Lizard. Athens, Ohio: Swallow Press, 1963.
The Orange Tree (chapbook). Chicago: Cyfoeth Press, 1965.
The Rainbow-Walker. Albuquerque: Grasshopper Press, 1969.
Dostoevsky And Other Nature Poems (chapbook). San Luis Obispo, Calif.: Solo Press, 1972.
Locust Cry: Poems 1958-1965. Cerrillos, N. Mex.: San Marcos Press, 1973.
The Mystic Writing-Pad. Fairfax, Calif.: Red Hill Press, 1977.
Loops (chapbook). Cerrillos, N. Mex.: San Marcos Press, 1978.
Clouds And Red Earth. Athens, Ohio: Swallow/Ohio University Press, 1981.
A Lover's Quarrel With America (chapbook). Albuquerque: Automatic Press, 1985.
A Sweetness In The Air. Atascadero, Calif.: Solo Press, 1987.

Joy Harjo

Born: Tulsa, Oklahoma, 9 May 1951.
Education: Institute of American Indian Arts, Santa Fe, High School Diploma, 1968. University of New Mexico, B.A., 1976. University of Iowa, M.F.A., 1978.
Career: New Mexico Poetry-in-the-Schools Program, artist-in-residence, 1974-1976, 1979-1980. Institute of American Indian Arts, Santa Fe, creative writing instructor, 1978-1979, 1983-1984. University of Colorado, Boulder, assistant professor, Department of English, 1985-present.
Awards: National Endowment for the Arts, Creative Writing Fellowship, 1978. Academy of American Poetry Award, University of New Mexico, 1976. Santa Fe Festival of the Arts Award for Poetry, 1980.
Residence: Denver, Colorado.

Selected Bibliography

The Last Song. Las Cruces, N. Mex.: Puerto del Sol Press, 1975.
What Moon Drove Me To This. Berkeley: I. Reed Books, 1980.
She Had Some Horses. New York: Thunder's Mouth Press, 1983.

Tony Hillerman

Born: Sacred Heart, Oklahoma, 27 May 1925.
Education: University of Oklahoma, B.A., Journalism. University of New Mexico, M.A., English.
Career: Police reporter. Political reporter. United Press International, New Mexico manager. *New Mexican* newspaper, editor. University of New Mexico, chairman, Journalism Department.
Awards: Dan Burrows Award for Investigative Reporting and Editorial Writing. Mystery Writers of America Edgar Allan Poe Award for Best Mystery Novel of 1973, *Dance Hall of the Dead*. Western Writers of America Award for Children's Literature. Border Regional Library Association Awards for *The Boy Who Made Dragonfly*, 1973, and *Rio Grande*, 1975. Festival International du Roman et du Film Noir, Le Gran Prix de Litterature Policiere, Grenoble, France, 1987. Navaho Nation, Friend of Dineh' Award, 1987.
Residence: Albuquerque, New Mexico.

Selected Bibliography

The Blessingway. New York: Harper and Row, 1970.
Fly On The Wall. New York: Harper and Row, 1971.
The Boy Who Made Dragonfly. New York: Harper and Row, 1972.
Dance Hall Of The Dead. New York: Harper and Row, 1973.
The Great Taos Bank Robbery. Albuquerque: University of New Mexico Press, 1973.
New Mexico (with David Muench). Portland, Oreg.: Graphic Arts Center Publishing Company, 1974.
Rio Grande (with Robert Reynolds). Portland, Oreg.: Graphic Arts Center Publishing Company, 1975.
The Spell of New Mexico. Albuquerque: University of New Mexico Press, 1976.
Listening Woman. New York: Harper and Row, 1978.
People Of Darkness. New York: Harper and Row, 1980.
The Dark Wind. New York: Harper and Row, 1982.
The Ghostway. New York: Harper and Row, 1984.
Skinwalker. New York: Harper and Row, 1986.
Indian Country. Flagstaff: Northland Press, 1987.
A Thief of Time. New York: Harper and Row, 1988.

Rolando Hinojosa-Smith

Born: Mercedes, Texas, 21 January 1929.
Education: University of Texas at Austin, B.S., 1953. New Mexico Highlands, M.A., 1963. University of Illinois, Ph.D., 1969.
Career: Trinity University, assistant professor, 1968-1970. Texas A.&I. University, associate professor, professor, vice president academic affairs, 1970-1977. University of Minnesota, professor of English, 1977-1981. University of Texas at Austin, Ellen Clayton Garwood Professor of English, 1985-present.
Awards: Quinto Sol Award, Best Novel for *Estampas*, 1982. Premio Casa de las Américas for *Klail City y sus alrededores*, 1976. Best Writing in Humanities, Conference on Latin American Studies, 1981.
Residence: Austin, Texas.

Selected Bibliography

Estampas del valle y otras abras. Berkeley: Quinto Sol Publications, 1973.
Klail City y sus alrededores. Havana, Cuba: Casa de las Américas, 1976.
Korean Love Songs. Berkeley: Editorial Justa, 1978.
Mi querido Rafa. Houston: Arte Público Press, 1981.
Rites and Witnesses. Houston: Arte Público Press, 1982.
The Valley. Ypsilanti, Mich.: Bilingual Press, Eastern Michigan University, 1983.
Dear Rafe. Houston: Arte Público Press, 1985.
Partners in Crime. Houston: Arte Público Press, 1985.
The Rolando Hinojosa Reader (edited by Jose Saldivar). Houston: Arte Público Press, 1985.
Claros varones de Belken. Binghamton, N.Y.: Bilingual Press, 1986.
Klail City. Houston: Arte Publico Press, 1987.
This Migrant Earth: Rolando Hinojosa's Rendition in English of Tomás Rivera's...y no se lo trago la tierra. Houston: Arte Público Press, 1987.

Paul Horgan

Born: Buffalo, New York, 1 August 1903.
Education: Nardin Academy, Buffalo. Albuquerque Public Schools, 1915. New Mexico Military Institute, 1919-1923.
Career: New Mexico Military Institute, librarian, 1926-1962. United States Army, 1942-1946. Wesleyan University, director, Center for Advanced Studies, 1962-1967; professor emeritus of English and permanent author-in-residence, 1969-present.
Awards: Harper Prize, *The Fault of Angels*, 1933. Guggenheim Fellowship, 1947 and 1958. Pulitzer Prize and Bancroft Prize, *Great River: The Rio Grande in North American History*, 1955. Pulitzer Prize, *Lamy of Santa Fe*, 1975. Notre Dame University, Laetare Medal, 1976. Wesleyan University, Baldwin Medal. Washington College, Washington Medal.
Residence: Middletown, Connecticut.

Selected Bibliography

Men Of Arms. Philadelphia: David McKay Company, 1931.
The Fault Of Angels. New York: Harper and Brothers, 1933.
No Quarter Given. New York: Harper and Brothers, 1935.
Main Line West. New York: Harper and Brothers, 1936.
The Return Of The Weed. New York: Harper and Brothers, 1936.
From The Royal City Of The Holy Faith Of St. Francis Of Assisi. Santa Fe: Rydal Press, 1936.
A Lamp On The Plains. New York: Harper and Brothers, 1937.
New Mexico's Own Chronicle (edited with Maurice Garland Fulton). Dallas: Banks Upshaw, 1937.
Far From Cibola. New York: Harper and Brothers, 1938.
The Habit of Empire. Santa Fe: Rydal Press, 1939.
Figures In A Landscape. New York: Harper and Brothers, 1940.
The Common Heart. New York: Harper and Brothers, 1942.
Look At America: The Southwest (and the editors of *Look*). Boston: Houghton Mifflin, 1947.
One Red Rose For Christmas. New York: Longmans, Green, 1950.
The Devil In The Desert. New York: Longmans, Green, 1952.
Great River: The Rio Grande In North American History. New York: Rinehart, 1954.
The Saintmaker's Christmas Eve. New York: Farrar, Straus, 1955.

Humble Powers. Ga. City, N.Y.: Doubleday, 1956.
The Centuries Of Santa Fe. N.Y.: Dutton, 1956.
Give Me Possession. New York: Farrar, Straus and Cudahy, 1957.
Rome Eternal. New York: Farrar, Straus, 1959.
A Distant Trumpet. New York: Farrar, Straus and Cudahy, 1960.
Citizen Of New Salem. New York: Farrar, Straus and Cudahy, 1961.
Mountain Standard Time. New York: Farrar, Straus and Cudahy, 1962.
Conquistadors In North American History. New York: Farrar, Straus and Company, 1963.
Toby And The Nighttime. New York: Farrar, Straus, 1963.
Things As They Are. New York: Farrar, Straus, 1964.
Songs After Lincoln. New York: Farrar, Straus and Giroux, 1965.
Peter Hurd, A Portrait Sketch From Life. Austin: University of Texas Press, 1965.
Memories Of The Future. New York: Farrar, Straus and Giroux, 1966.
The Peach Stone: Stories From Four Decades. New York: Farrar, Straus and Giroux, 1967.
Everything To Live For. New York: Farrar, Straus and Giroux, 1968.
The Heroic Triad. New York: Holt, Rinehart and Winston, 1970.
Whitewater. New York: Farrar, Straus and Giroux, 1970.
Maurice Baring Restored. New York: Farrar, Straus and Giroux, 1970.
Encounters With Stravinsky. New York: Farrar, Straus and Giroux, 1972.
Approaches To Writing. New York: Farrar, Straus and Giroux, 1973.
Lamy Of Santa Fe. New York: Farrar, Straus and Giroux, 1975.
The Thin Mountain Air. New York: Farrar, Straus and Giroux, 1977.
Josiah Gregg And His Vision Of The Early West. New York: Farrar, Straus and Giroux, 1979.
Mexico Bay. New York: Farrar, Straus and Giroux, 1982.
A Gallery Of Clerihews. Middletown, Conn.: Piratical Primrose Press, 1984.
The Annotated Clerihew. Middletown, Conn.: Piratical Primrose Press, 1984.
Of America East And West. New York: Farrar, Straus and Giroux, 1984.
Under The Sangre De Cristo. Santa Fe: Rydal Press, 1985.
The Clerihews Of Paul Horgan. Middletown, Conn.: Wesleyan University Press, 1985.

Dorothy B. Hughes

Born: Kansas City, Missouri, 10 August 1904. Dorothy Belle Flanagan.
Education: University of Missouri, B.J., 1924. Graduate studies, Columbia University, University of New Mexico, University of California at Los Angeles.
Career: Taught at University of New Mexico and University of California at Los Angeles. Newspaper columnist (mystery criticism) for forty years.
Awards: Mystery Writers of America Edgar For Best Criticism, 1955; Scroll for *The Expendable Man,* 1963; Edgar, Grand Master Award, 1978; Scroll for *Erle Stanley Gardner,* 1979. Swedish Academy of Crime, Grand Master Award, 1981.
Residence: Newport Beach, California.

Selected Bibliography

Dark Certainty. New Haven: Yale University Press, 1931.
Pueblo On The Mesa: The First Forty Years At The University Of New Mexico. Albuquerque: University of New Mexico Press, 1939.
The So Blue Marble. New York: Duell, Sloan and Pearce, 1940.
The Cross-Eyed Bear. New York: Duell, Sloan and Pearce, 1940.

The Bamboo Blond. New York: Duell, Sloan and Pearce, 1941.
The Fallen Sparrow. New York: Duell, Sloan and Pearce, 1942.
The Blackbirder. New York: Duell, Sloan and Pearce, 1943.
The Delicate Ape. New York: Duell, Sloan and Pearce, 1944.
Johnnie. New York: Duell, Sloan and Pearce, 1944.
Dread Journey. New York: Duell, Sloan and Pearce, 1945.
Ride The Pink Horse. New York: Duell, Sloan and Pearce, 1946.
In A Lonely Place. New York: Duell, Sloan and Pearce, 1947.
The Big Barbecue. New York: Random House, 1949.
The Candy Kid. New York: Duell, Sloan and Pearce, 1950.
The Davidian Report. New York: Duell, Sloan and Pearce, 1952.
The Expendable Man. New York: Random House, 1963.
Erle Stanley Gardner: The Case Of The Real Perry Mason. New York: William Morrow, 1978.

Arturo Islas

Born: El Paso, Texas, 24 May 1938.
Education: Stanford University, A.B., 1960; M.A., 1963; Ph.D., 1970.
Career: Stanford University, assistant professor, 1971; associate professor, 1976; professor of Literature, 1985-present.
Awards: Phi Beta Kappa, 1960. Dinkelspiel Award, Stanford University, 1976. Stanford University Fellow, 1979-1981. Border Regional Library Association Award, *The Rain God,* 1986.
Residence: Stanford, California.

Selected Bibliography

The Rain God. Palo Alto, Calif.: Alexandrian Press, 1984.
La Mollie and the King of Tears.
Migrant Souls.

Elmer Kelton

Born: Five Wells Ranch, Andrews County, Texas, 29 April 1926.
Education: University of Texas at Austin, B.A., Journalism, 1948.
Career: San Angelo *Standard-Times,* farm and ranch writer, 1948-1963. *Sheep and Goat Raiser Magazine,* editor, 1963-1968. *Livestock Weekly,* associate editor, 1968-present.
Awards: Western Writers of America, Spur Awards for *Buffalo Wagons,* 1956, *The Day the Cowboys Quit,* 1971, *The Time It Never Rained,* 1973, *Eyes of the Hawk,* 1981. National Cowboy Hall of Fame, Western Heritage Awards for *The Time It Never Rained,* 1973, *The Good Old Boys,* 1978. Texas Institute of Letters, Barbara McCombs/Lon Tinkle Award, 1987.
Residence: San Angelo, Texas.

Selected Bibliography

Hot Iron. New York: Ballantine Books, 1955.
Buffalo Wagons. New York: Ballantine Books, 1956.
Barbed Wire. New York: Ballantine Books, 1957.
Shadow of A Star. New York: Ballantine Books, 1959.
The Texas Rifles. New York: Ballantine Books, 1960.

Donovan. New York: Ballantine Books, 1961.
Bitter Trail. New York: Ballantine Books, 1962.
Horsehead Crossing. New York: Ballantine Books, 1963.
Massacre at Goliad. New York: Ballantine Books, 1965.
Llano River. New York: Ballantine Books, 1966.
After the Bugles. New York: Ballantine Books, 1967.
Captain's Rangers. New York: Ballantine Books, 1968.
Hanging Judge. New York: Ballantine Books, 1969.
Bowie's Mine. New York: Ballantine Books, 1971.
The Day The Cowboys Quit. Garden City, N.Y.: Doubleday, 1971.
Wagontongue. New York: Ballantine Books, 1972.
Looking Back West. San Angelo, Tex.: Tally Press, 1972.
The Time It Never Rained. Garden City, N.Y.: Doubleday, 1973.
Manhunters. New York: Ballantine Books, 1974.
The Good Old Boys. Garden City, N.Y.: Doubleday, 1978.
The Wolf and the Buffalo. Garden City, N.Y.: Doubleday, 1980.
Frank C. McCarthy: The Old West. Trumbell, Conn.: Greenwich Press, 1981.
Stand Proud. Garden City, N.Y.: Doubleday, 1984.
Dark Thicket. Garden City, N.Y.: Doubleday, 1985.
Permian, A Continuing Saga. Midland, Tex.: Permian Basin Petroleum Museum, 1986.
The Big Brand. New York: Bantam Books, 1986.
There's Always Another Chance. San Angelo, Tex.: Fort Concho Museum Press, 1986.
The Man Who Rode Midnight. Garden City, N.Y.: Doubleday, 1987.

As Alex Hawk:
Shotgun Settlement. New York: Paperback Library, 1969.

As Lee McElroy:
Joe Pepper. Garden City, N.Y.: Doubleday, 1975.
Long Way To Texas. Garden City, N.Y.: Doubleday, 1976.
Eyes of the Hawk. Garden City, N.Y.: Doubleday, 1981.

David Lavender

Born: Telluride, Colorado, 4 February 1910.
Education: Princeton University, A.B., 1931. Stanford University Law School, 1931-1932.
Career: Miner, Camp Bird gold mine, Ouray, Colorado. Rancher. Advertising copywriter, Denver, Colorado. Thacher School for Boys, Ojai, California, instructor, head, English Department.
Awards: Two Guggenheim Fellowships. Three Commonwealth Club of California medals. Two Pulitzer Prize nominations. Western Writers of America, Spur Award.
Residence: Ojai, California.

Selected Bibliography

One Man's West. Garden City, N.Y.: Doubleday, 1943.
Trouble At Tamarack. Philadelphia: Westminster Press, 1943.
Mike Maroney, Raider. Philadelphia: Westminster Press, 1945.
Andy Claybourne. Garden City, N.Y.: Doubleday, 1946.
The Big Divide. Garden City, N.Y.: Doubleday, 1948.
Golden Trek. Philadelphia: Westminster Press, 1948.
Bent's Fort. Garden City, N.Y.: Doubleday, 1954.
Land of Giants, The Drive To The Pacific Northwest, 1750-1950. Garden City, N.Y.: Doubleday, 1956.

The Trail To Santa Fe. New York: Houghton Mifflin, 1958.
The Story Of Cyprus Mines Corporation. San Marino, Calif.: The Huntington Library, 1962.
Red Mountain. Garden City, N.Y.: Doubleday, 1963.
Westward Vision, The Story Of The Oregon Trail. New York: McGraw Hill, 1963.
Fist In The Wilderness. Garden City, N.Y.: Doubleday, 1964.
The American Heritage History Of The Great West. New York: American Heritage Publishing Company, 1965.
Climax At Buena Vista. New York: J.P. Lippincott, 1966.
The Rockies. New York: Harper and Row, 1968.
The Story of California. New York: Harper and Row and American Heritage Publishing Company, 1969.
The Great Persuader. Garden City, N.Y.: Doubleday, 1970.
California, Land of New Beginnings. New York: Harper and Row, 1972.
Nothing Seemed Impossible: William Ralston and Early San Francisco. Palo Alto, Calif.: American West Publishing Company, 1975.
David Lavender's Colorado. Garden City, N.Y.: Doubleday, 1976.
California, A Bicentennial History. New York: W.W. Norton, 1976.
Winner Take All. New York: McGraw Hill, 1977.
The Southwest. New York: Harper and Row, 1980.
The Overland Migrations, Settlers To Oregon, California And Utah. Washington, D.C.: National Park Service, United States Department of the Interior, 1980.
Los Angeles Two Hundred. Tulsa, Okla.: Continental Heritage Press, 1980.
Fort Vancouver. Washington, D.C.: National Park Service, United States Department of the Interior, 1981.
Colorado River Country. New York: E.P. Dutton, 1982.
Fort Laramie And The Changing Frontier. Washington, D.C.: National Park Service, United States Department of the Interior, 1983.
River Runners of the Grand Canyon. Tucson: University of Arizona Press and the Grand Canyon National History Association, 1985.
Images From the Southwest (with Marc Gaede). Flagstaff: Northland Press, 1986.
The Telluride Story. Ouray, Colo.: Wayfinder Press, 1987.
The Way To the Western Sea: Lewis and Clark Across the Continent. New York: Harper and Row, 1988.

Tom Lea

Born: El Paso, Texas, 11 July 1907.
Education: Art Institute of Chicago, 1924-1926. Student in Italy, 1930.
Career: Mural painter, commercial artist, art teacher, Chicago, 1926-1933. Laboratory of Anthropology, Santa Fe, staff, 1933-1935. Muralist, easel painter, book illustrator, El Paso, 1936-present. *Life* magazine, war correspondent, 1941-1946.
Awards: Baylor University, Litt. D., 1967. Southern Methodist University, L.H.D., 1970.

Residence: El Paso, Texas.

Selected Bibliography
Randado. El Paso: Hertzog, 1941.
A Grizzly From The Coral Sea: Conversation And Pictures. El Paso: Hertzog, 1944.
Peleliu Landing. El Paso: Hertzog, 1945.
Twelve Travellers. El Paso: Hertzog, 1947.
Fort Bliss: One Hundredth Anniversary. El Paso: Guynes, 1948.

Bullfight Manual For Spectators. El Paso: Hertzog, 1949.
The Brave Bulls. Boston: Little, Brown and Company, 1949.
The Wonderful Country. Boston: Little, Brown and Company, 1952.
The King Ranch. Boston: Little, Brown and Company, 1957.
The Primal Yoke. Boston: Little, Brown and Company, 1960.
The Hands Of Cantú. Boston: Little, Brown and Company, 1964.
A Picture Gallery. Boston: Little, Brown and Company, 1968.
In The Crucible Of The Sun. Kingsville, Tex.: King Ranch, 1974.

Harold Littlebird

Born: Albuquerque, New Mexico, 28 May 1951.
Education: Graduate, Institute of American Indian Arts, 1969.
Career: Performing poet, songwriter, ceramicist, 1969-present.
Awards: Vincent Price Poetry Award, 1969. National Endowment for the Arts Crafts Fellowship, 1980. Southwestern Association on Indian Affairs Fellow, 1983. Rio Grande Institute Fellowship, 1985. Katrin H. Lamon Fellowship, School of American Research, 1986-1987.
Residence: Santa Fe, New Mexico.

Selected Bibliography

On Mountains' Breath. Corrales, N.Mex.: Tooth of Time Press, 1982.
A Circle Begins (tape). Santa Fe: Littlebird Studios, 1985.
The Road Back In (tape). Santa Fe: Littlebird Studios, 1987.

Mark Medoff

Born: Mt. Carmel, Illinois, 18 March 1940.
Education: University of Miami, B.A. Stanford University, M.A.
Career: Professional playwright, screenwriter, director, and actor. New Mexico State University, Las Cruces, professor of Drama and English, 1966-present; head, Department of Theatre Arts, 1978-1983, 1985-1987. American Southwest Theatre Company, Las Cruces, New Mexico, artistic director, 1984-1987.
Awards: For *Red Ryder: Best Plays 1973-1974,* Outer Critics Award, Drama Desk Award, Obie Award for Distinguished Playwriting. New Mexico State University, Westhafer Award for Excellence in Creative Activity, 1974. *Best Plays 1974-1975, The Wager.* Guggenheim Fellowship in Playwriting, 1974-1975. *Best Short Plays, Doing A Good One For The Red Man,* 1975. Nominated, Best New Play, *The Conversion Of Aaron Weiss,* American Theatre Critics Association, 1977-1978. New Mexico Governor's Award for Excellence in the Arts, 1980. For *Children Of A Lesser God:* Antoinette Perry Award (The Tony) for Best Play, 1979-1980 Season; Drama Desk for Best Play; New York Outer Critics' Circle Award for Best Play of the New York Season; Los Angeles *Drama-Logue* Critics' Award for Playwriting; Society of West End Theatres, Best Play, 1981 Season; Academy Award nomination for screenplay, 1987. El Paso Herald-Post Writers Hall of Fame, Inductee, 1987.
Residence: Las Cruces, New Mexico.

Selected Bibliography

PLAYS

When You Comin Back, Red Ryder? New York: Dramatists Play Service and Clifton, N.J.: James T. White and Company, 1974.
The Wager. New York: Dramatists Play Service and Clifton, N.J.: James T. White and Company, 1975.
Four Short Plays. New York: Dramatists Play Service, 1974.
The Kramer. New York: Dramatists Play Service, 1974.
The Odyssey Of Jeremy Jack (with Carleene Johnson). New York: Dramatists Play Service, 1975.
The Halloween Bandit. 1978.
The Conversion of Aaron Weiss. 1978.
Firekeeper. 1978.
The Last Chance Saloon. 1979.
Children Of A Lesser God. Clifton, N.J.: James T. White and Company, 1979.
The Majestic Kid. New York: Dramatists Play Service, 1981.
The Hands Of Its Enemy. 1984.
Kringle's Window. 1985.
The Heart Outright. 1986.
The Homage That Follows. 1987.

RADIO PLAYS

The Last Chance Saloon. 1979.
The Disintegration Of Aaron Weiss. 1979.

FILMS

Good Guys Wear Black. Mar Vista Productions, 1978.
When You Comin Back, Red Ryder? Columbia Pictures, 1979.
Off Beat. Disney Studios, 1986.
Apology. Home Box Office Premiere, 1986.
Children Of A Lesser God. Paramount, 1986.
Clara's Heart. Warner Brothers, 1987.

Leon C. Metz

Born: Parkersburg, West Virginia, 6 November 1930.
Career: United States Air Force, 1948-1952. Standard Oil Refinery, El Paso, operator, 1953-1967. University of Texas at El Paso, University archivist, 1967-1979; assistant to President Haskell Monroe, 1981-1984. Executive assistant to El Paso Mayor Tom Westfall, 1979-1981. MBank El Paso, public affairs officer, 1984-1987.
Awards: Texas Institute of Letters Award for Biography, *John Selman,* 1966. Border Regional Library Association Awards, *Pat Garrett,* 1976; *Fort Bliss,* 1982. Texas Historical Commission Award, *Fort Bliss,* 1982. Western Writers of America, Saddleman Award, 1985. El Paso Herald-Post Writers Hall of Fame, Inductee, 1988.

Residence: El Paso, Texas.

Selected Bibliography

John Selman: Gunfighter. New York: Hastings House, 1966.
Dallas Stoudenmire: El Paso Marshal. Austin: Pemberton Press, 1969.
Pat Garrett: The Story of a Western Lawman. Norman: University of Oklahoma, 1974.
The Shooters. El Paso: Mangan Books, 1976.
City At The Pass: An Illustrated History Of El Paso. Woodland Hills, Calif.: Windsor Publications, 1980.
Fort Bliss: An Illustrated History. El Paso: Mangan Books, 1981.
Turning Points In El Paso, Texas. El Paso: Mangan Books, 1985.

N. Scott Momaday

Born: Lawton, Oklahoma, 27 February 1934.
Education: University of New Mexico, B.A., Political Science, 1958. Stanford University, M.A., 1960, Ph.D., 1963.
Career: University of California at Santa Barbara, instructor, English and Comparative Literature, 1963-1969. University of California at Berkeley, instructor, 1969-1972. New Mexico State University, Distinguished Visiting Professor of Humanities, 1972-1973. University of Moscow, instructor, 1974. Stanford University, professor of English and Comparative Literature, 1973-1981. University of Arizona, professor of English, 1981-1987.
Awards: Stanford University, Creative Writing Fellowship, 1959. Guggenheim Scholarship, 1966-1967. Pulitzer Prize, *House Made of Dawn,* 1969. Eight honorary doctoral degrees.
Residence: Tucson, Arizona.

Selected Bibliography

The Complete Poems Of Frederick Goodard Tuckerman (editor). New York: Oxford University Press, 1965.
The Journey Of Tai-Me. Santa Barbara: Privately printed, 1967.
House Made Of Dawn. New York: Harper and Row, 1968.
The Way To Rainy Mountain. Albuquerque: University of New Mexico Press, 1969.
Colorado: Summer, Fall, Winter And Spring. New York: Rand McNally, 1973.
Angle Of Geese And Other Poems. Boston: David R. Godine, 1974.
The Gourd Dancer. New York: Harper and Row, 1976.
The Names: A Memoir. New York: Harper and Row, 1976.

Pat Mora

Born: El Paso, Texas, 19 January 1942.
Education: Texas Western College, B.A., English/Speech, 1963. University of Texas at El Paso, M.A., English/Speech, 1967.
Career: Taught English for El Paso Public Schools, El Paso Community College. The University of Texas at El Paso, taught English; assistant to the vice president for Academic Affairs, 1981-present; El Paso Centennial Museum, interim director, 1987-1988.
Awards: National Association for Chicano Studies, Creative Writing Award, 1983. Southwest Council of Latin American Studies, Harvey L. Johnson Book Award, Literary Award, 1984. Border Regional Library Association Awards, *Chants,* 1984; *Borders,* 1986. W.K. Kellogg National Fellowship Award, 1986. Elected to Texas Institute of Letters, 1987. El Paso Herald-Post Writers Hall of Fame, Inductee, 1988.
Residence: El Paso, Texas.

Selected Bibliography

Chants. Houston: Arte Público Press, 1984.
Borders. Houston: Arte Público Press, 1986.

Gary Paul Nabhan

Born: Gary, Indiana, 17 March 1952.
Education: Cornell College, Iowa, and Prescott College, Arizona, B.A. with honors. University of Arizona, M.S., Ph.D. Learned much from native farmers in Arizona, Sonora, Chihuahua and New Mexico.
Career: University of Arizona, research faculty. Native Seeds/SEARCH, non-profit genetic conservation organization, co-founder. Desert Botanical Garden, Phoenix, assistant director for Research and Collections. Ethnobotanist. Agroecologist. Conservationist.
Awards: John Burroughs Medal, Best Nature Book, 1986. Border Regional Library Association, *Gathering the Desert,* 1987.
Residence: Tempe, Arizona.

Selected Bibliography

The Desert Smells Like Rain: A Naturalist In Papago Indian Country. San Francisco: North Point Press, 1982.
Gathering The Desert. Tucson: University of Arizona Press, 1985.
Saguaro: A Naturalist's View of Saguaro National Monument. Tucson: Southwest Parks and Monuments Association, 1986.
Enduring Seeds: Native American Agriculture and Wild Plant Conservation. San Francisco: North Point Press, 1988.

John Nichols

Born: Berkeley, California, 23 July 1940.
Education: Hamilton College, Clinton, New York, B.A., 1962.
Career: Writer, screenwriter, photographer.
Awards: New Mexico Governor's Award for Excellence in Literature, 1981.
Residence: Taos, New Mexico.

Selected Bibliography

The Sterile Cuckoo. New York: David McKay, 1965.
The Wizard Of Loneliness. New York: G.P. Putnam's Sons, 1966.
The Milagro Beanfield War. New York: Holt, Rinehart and Winston, 1974.
The Magic Journey. New York: Holt, Rinehart and Winston, 1978.
A Ghost In The Music. New York: Holt, Rinehart and Winston, 1979.
If Mountains Die. New York: Alfred Knopf, 1979.
The Nirvana Blues. New York: Holt, Rinehart and Winston, 1981.
The Last Beautiful Days Of Autumn. New York: Holt, Rinehart and Winston, 1982.
On The Mesa. Salt Lake City: Peregrine Smith, 1986.
American Blood. New York: Henry Holt and Company, 1987.
A Fragile Beauty. Salt Lake City: Peregrine Smith, 1987.

Stanley Noyes

Born: San Francisco, California, 1924.
Education: University of California, Berkeley, B.A., English, 1950; M.A., English, 1951.
Career: California College of Arts and Crafts, Oakland, taught English and writing, 1953-1961. College of Santa Fe, taught English and Writing, 1965-1971. *New Mexico Magazine,* poetry editor, 1973-1977. New Mexico Arts Division, Literary Arts coordinator, 1972-1986.
Awards: MacDowell Colony Grant, Peterborough, New Hampshire, 1967.
Residence: Santa Fe, New Mexico.

Selected Bibliography

No Flowers For A Clown. New York: Macmillan Company, 1961.
Shadowbox. New York: Macmillan Company, 1970.
Faces And Spirits. Santa Fe: 1974.
Beyond The Mountains Beyond The Mountains. San Luis Obispo, Calif.: Solo Press, 1979.
Western (chapbook). Cerrillos, N. Mex.: San Marcos Press, 1980.
The Commander Of Dead Leaves. Santa Fe: Tooth of Time, 1984.

Lawrence Clark Powell

Born: Washington, D.C., 3 September 1906.
Education: Occidental College, A.B., 1928. University of Dijon, Ph.D., 1932. University of California, Berkeley, M.L.S., 1937.
Career: University of California at Los Angeles, chief administrator of the William Andrews Clark Memorial Library; University librarian; founder, School of Library Services; dean, Graduate Library School, 1938-1966. University of Arizona, professor in residence, 1971-present.
Awards: Guggenheim Fellowship, 1950, 1966. American Library Association, First Clarence Day Award, 1960. California Historical Society Fellow, 1975. University of San Francisco, Sir Thomas More Medal, 1977. Southern Methodist University, DeGolyer Medal, 1987. Several honorary doctorates.
Residence: Tucson, Arizona.

Selected Bibliography

Robinson Jeffers: The Man And His Work. Los Angeles: Primavera Press, 1934.
The Manuscripts of D.H. Lawrence. Los Angeles: Los Angeles Public Library, 1937.
Philosopher Pickett. Berkeley: University of California Press, 1942.
Islands Of Books. Los Angeles: Ward Ritchie Press, 1951.
Land Of Fiction. Los Angeles: Glen Dawson, 1952.
The Alchemy Of Books. Los Angeles: Ward Ritchie Press, 1954.
Heart Of The Southwest. Los Angeles: Dawson's Bookshop, 1955.
Books West Southwest. Los Angeles: Ward Ritchie Press, 1957.
A Southwestern Century. Van Nuys, Calif.: J.E. Reynolds, Bookseller, 1958.
The Malibu. Los Angeles: Dawson's Bookshop, 1958.
A Passion For Books. Cleveland: World Publishing Company, 1959.

Books In My Baggage. Cleveland: World Publishing Company, 1960.
Southwestern Book Trails. Albuquerque: Horn and Wallace, Publishers, 1963.
Leaves of Grass (editor). New York: Crowell Company, 1963.
The Little Package. Cleveland: World Publishing Company, 1964.
Bibliographers Of The Golden State. Los Angeles: University of California, 1967.
Bookman's Progress. Los Angeles: Ward Ritchie Press, 1968.
Fortune and Friendship: An Autobiography. New York: R.R. Bowker Company, 1968.
California Classics. Los Angeles: Ward Ritchie Press, 1971.
Southwest Classics. Los Angeles: Ward Ritchie Press, 1974.
Desert Splendor. Phoenix: Arizona Highways, 1975.
Arizona: A Bicentennial History. New York: W.W. Norton and Company, 1976.
From The Heartland. Flagstaff: Northland Press, 1976.
The Blue Train. Santa Barbara: Capra Press, 1977.
The River Between. Santa Barbara: Capra Press, 1979.
Where Water Flows: The Rivers Of Arizona (with Michael Collier). Flagstaff: Northland Press, 1980.
El Morro. Santa Barbara: Capra Press, 1984.
Books Are Basic: The Essential Lawrence Clark Powell (edited by J.D. Marshall). Tucson: University of Arizona Press, 1985.
Life Goes On: Twenty More Years of Fortune and Friendship. Metuchen, N.J.: Scarecrow Press, 1986.
Portrait of My Father. Santa Barbara: Capra Press, 1986.

Jim Sagel

Born: Fort Morgan, Colorado, 19 June 1947.
Education: University of Colorado, B.A., English, 1970. University of New Mexico, M.A., English, 1976.
Career: Teacher, Espanola Public Schools, Espanola, New Mexico, 1972-1981; instructor, Northern Branch of the University of New Mexico and Northern New Mexico Community College, Espanola, New Mexico, 1976-present. *Conexiones Poéticas,* co-translator in project supported by the Witter Bynner Foundation to translate contemporary Mexican poets into English, 1983-1984. Correspondent, *Albuquerque Journal* and *Hispanic Link,* 1981-present. New Mexico Arts Division, Artists in Residence Program, 1981-present.
Awards: Poetry in Public Places, New York City, 1979. Premio Casa de las Américas, *Tunomás Honey,* 1981. New Mexico Governor's Award, *Santa Cruz de la Canada, 1733-1983,* 1984.
Residence: Espanola, New Mexico.

Selected Bibliography

Hablando de brujas (y la gente de antes). Austin: Place of Herons Press, 1981.
Foreplay and French Fries. San Jose, Calif.: Mango Publications, 1981.
Tunomás Honey. Havana, Cuba: Premio Casa de las Américas, 1981.
Small Bones/Little Eyes. Fallon, Nev.: Duck Down Press, 1982.
Tunomas Honey (bilingual edition). Tempe, Ariz.: Bilingual Press, 1983.
Los Cumpleaños de Doña Agueda. Austin: Place of Herons Press, 1984.
Mas Que No Love it. El Paso: Dos Pasos Editores, 1987.
Sábelotodo Entiendelonada. Tempe, Ariz.: Bilingual Press, 1988.

Ricardo Sánchez

Born: El Paso, Texas, 29 March 1941.
Education: Union Graduate School, Cincinnati, Ohio, Ph.D., American Studies and Ethnic Cultural History and Poetics.
Career: Freelance writer, poet, speaker, performer. Bookstore owner, PAPERBACKS . . . ¡y Mas!, San Antonio. The Poets of Tejas Reading Series, founder, director. *San Antonio Express News,* Sunday arts columnist. Consultant on cross-cultural phenomena, incarceration, community organizing, proposal writing, Chicano literature and aesthetics, and social and arts program development.
Awards: Ford Foundation, Frederick Douglass Fellowship in Journalism, 1969-1970; Graduate Fellowship, 1973-1975. University of Utah at Salt Lake City, Outstanding Faculty Member. Tribute to the Chicano Arts, Award for Excellence in programming for Poets of Tejas, Centro Cultural Aztlan, San Antonio.
Residence: San Antonio, Texas.

Selected Bibliography

Canto y Grito mi Liberación. El Paso: Mictla Publications, 1971.
Los Cuatro. Denver: Barrio Press, 1971.
Hechizospells. Los Angeles: Chicano Studies Center, University of California at Los Angeles, 1976.
Canto al Pueblo. San Antonio: Penca Books, 1978.
Milhuas Blues y Gritos Norteños. Milwaukee: University of Wisconsin, 1978.
Brown Bear Honey Madness: Alaskan Cruising Poems. Austin: Slough Press, 1981.
Amsterdam Cantos y Poemas Pistos. Austin: Place of Herons, 1983.
Perdido. Austin: R.E.M. Publications, 1986.
Selected Poems. Houston: Arte Público Press, 1986.

Jack Schaefer

Born: Cleveland, Ohio, 19 November 1907.
Education: Oberlin College, A.B., 1929. Columbia University, postgraduate studies, 1929-1930.
Career: United Press, reporter, 1930-1931. Connecticut State Reformatory, assistant director of education, 1931-1938. New Haven *Journal Courier,* associate editor, 1932-1939; editor, 1939-1942. Baltimore *Sun,* editorial writer, 1942-1944. Norfolk *Virginian-Pilot,* associate editor, 1944-1948. *Theatre News,* editor and publisher, 1935-1940. *The Movies,* editor and publisher, 1939-1941.
Awards: Western Literature Association, Distinguished Achievement Award, 1975. Western Writers of America, Saddleman Award, 1986.
Residence: Santa Fe, New Mexico.

Selected Bibliography

Shane. Boston: Houghton Mifflin Company, 1949.
The Big Range. Boston: Houghton Mifflin Company, 1953.
The Canyon. Boston: Houghton Mifflin Company, 1953.
First Blood. Boston: Houghton Mifflin Company, 1953.
The Pioneers. Boston: Houghton Mifflin Comnany, 1954.
Out West: An Anthology of Stories. Boston: Houghton Mifflin Company, 1955.

Company of Cowards. Boston: Houghton Mifflin Company, 1957.
The Kean Land And Other Stories. Boston: Houghton Mifflin Company, 1959.
Old Ramon. Boston: Houghton Mifflin Company, 1960.
The Great Endurance Horse Race. Santa Fe: Stagecoach Press, 1963.
Monte Walsh. Boston: Houghton Mifflin Company, 1963.
The Plainsmen. Boston: Houghton Mifflin Company, 1963.
Stubby Pringle's Christmas. Boston: Houghton Mifflin Company, 1964.
Heroes Without Glory: Some Good Men Of The Old West. Boston: Houghton Mifflin Company, 1965.
Adolphe Francis Alphonse Bandelier. Santa Fe: Territorian Press, 1966.
The Collected Stories Of Jack Schaefer. Boston: Houghton Mifflin Company, 1966.
Mavericks. Boston: Houghton Mifflin Company, 1967.
New Mexico. States of the Nation Series. New York: Coward-McCann, 1967.
The Short Novels Of Jack Schaefer. Boston: Houghton Mifflin Company, 1967.
An American Bestiary. Boston: Houghton Mifflin Company, 1975.
Conversations With A Pocket Gopher, And Other Outspoken Neighbors. Santa Barbara: Capra Press, 1978.

Marc Simmons

Born: Dallas, Texas, 1937.
Education: University of Texas, Austin, B.A., 1958. University of New Mexico, Albuquerque, M.A., 1960, Ph.D., 1965.
Career: Professional historian and author. Awards: Woodrow Wilson Fellow. Guggenheim Fellow. Border Regional Library Association Award and Western Writers of America, Golden Spur for *Albuquerque.* Texas Western Press, C.L. Sonnichsen Award, *Murder On The Santa Fe Trail,* 1986. Border Regional Library Award, *Along the Santa Fe Trail,* 1987.
Residence: Cerrillos, New Mexico.

Selected Bibliography

Border Comanches: Seven Spanish Colonial Documents, 1785-1819. Santa Fe: Stagecoach Press, 1967.
Turquoise And Six Guns: The Story Of Cerrillos, New Mexico. Cerrillos, N. Mex.: Galisteo Press, 1968.
Spanish Government In New Mexico. Albuquerque: University of New Mexico, 1968.
The Fighting Settlers of Seboyeta. Cerrillos, N. Mex.: San Marcos Press, 1971.
Opening The Santa Fe Trail. Cerrillos, N. Mex.: Marc Simmons, 1971.
Little Lion Of The Southwest: A Life Of Manuel Antonio Chaves. Chicago: Swallow Press, 1973.
Witchcraft In The Southwest: Spanish And Indian Supernaturalism On The Rio Grande. Flagstaff: Northland Press, 1974.
Account Of Disorders In New Mexico. Isleta Pueblo, N. Mex.: Historical Society of New Mexico, 1977.
New Mexico: A History. New York: W.W. Norton and Company, 1977.
Taos To Tomé: True Tales Of Hispanic New Mexico. Albuquerque: Adobe Press, 1978.
People Of The Sun. Albuquerque: University of New Mexico Press, 1979.
Southwestern Colonial Ironwork: The Spanish Blacksmithing Tradition From Texas To California. Santa Fe: Museum of New Mexico Press, 1980.
Albuquerque: A Narrative History. Albuquerque: University of New Mexico Press, 1982.

New Mexico! Salt Lake City: Peregrine Smith Books, 1983.
Ranchers, Ramblers and Renegades: True Tales of Territorial New Mexico. Santa Fe: Ancient City Press, 1984.
Following the Santa Fe Trail: A Guide For Modern Travelers. Santa Fe: Ancient City Press, 1984.
Along the Santa Fe Trail. Albuquerque: University of New Mexico Press, 1986.
On The Santa Fe Trail. Lawrence, Kans.: University Press of Kansas, 1986.
Murder On The Santa Fe Trail, An International Incident, 1843. El Paso: Texas Western Press, 1987.
The Battle At Valley's Ranch. Cedar Crest, N. Mex.: San Pedro Press, 1987.

John L. Sinclair

Born: New York, New York, 6 December 1902.
Education: Attended private schools in England. Studied agriculture in Scotland.
Career: Drumlanrig Castle, Scotland, agricultural apprentice, 1919-1923. Southern New Mexico, cowboy, 1923-1937. Museum of New Mexico, Santa Fe, research assistant, 1938-1940. Lincoln County Museum, Lincoln, New Mexico, curator, 1940-1942. Coronado State Monument, New Mexico, superintendent, 1944-1946, 1947-1962.
Awards: Western Writers of America, Golden Spur Award, 1978. Cowboy Hall of Fame, Western Heritage Wrangler Award, 1978, 1986. National Cowboy Hall of Fame and Western Heritage Center, Honorary Life Member, 1978.
Residence: Bernalillo, New Mexico.

Selected Bibliography

In Time Of Harvest. New York: Macmillan Company, 1943.
Death In The Claimshack. Denver: Sage Books, 1947.
Profile Of A State (with George Fitzpatrick). Albuquerque: Horn and Wallace, 1964.
Cousin Drewey And The Holy Twister. Frenchtown, N.J.: Columbia Publishing Company, 1980.
New Mexico, Shining Land. Albuquerque: University of New Mexico, 1980.
Cowboy Riding Country. Albuquerque: University of New Mexico, 1982.

Joseph Somoza

Born: Verina, Asturias, Spain, 30 October 1940.
Education: University of Cincinnati, B.A., English, 1963. Roosevelt University, M.A., English, 1966. University of Iowa, M.F.A., Creative Writing, 1973.
Career: University of Texas at El Paso, English instructor, 1966-1968. University of Puerto Rico, Cayey, English instructor, 1969-1971. New Mexico State University, Las Cruces, English instructor, assistant professor, associate professor, 1973-present.
Residence: Las Cruces, New Mexico.

Selected Bibliography

Greyhound. Sacramento: Grande Ronde Press, 1968.
Olive Women. Cerrillos, N. Mex.: San Marcos Press, 1977.
Backyard Poems. El Paso: Cinco Puntos Press, 1986.

C.L. Sonnichsen

Born: Fonda, Iowa, 20 September 1901.
Education: University of Minnesota, B.A., 1924. Harvard University, M.A., 1927; Ph.D., 1931.
Career: St. James School, Faribault, Minnesota, assistant master, 1924-1926. Carnegie Institute of Technology, instructor, English, 1927-1929. University of Texas at El Paso (first known as Texas College of Mines then Texas Western College), associate professor, 1931-1933; professor, chairman, Department of English, 1933-1960; dean Graduate School, 1960-1967; H.Y. Benedict Professor, 1968-1972; professor emeritus, 1972-present. *Journal of Arizona History*, director of publications, editor, 1972-1977; senior editor, 1977-present.
Awards: University of Oklahoma, Rockefeller Fellowship, 1949-1950. Texas State Historical Association Fellow. University of Texas at El Paso, Minnie Stevens Piper Professorship, 1971. Cowboy Hall of Fame, Wrangler Award, 1975. Western Writers of America, Spur Award, 1975, 1977; Saddleman Award, 1980. Western History Association, Award of Merit, 1979. Association for State and Local History, 1979. El Paso Herald-Post Writers Hall of Fame, Inductee, 1986.
Residence: Tucson, Arizona.

Selected Bibliography

Billy King's Tombstone. Caldwell, Idaho: Caxton Printers, 1942.
Roy Bean: Law West Of The Pecos. New York: Macmillan Company, 1943.
Cowboys and Cattle Kings. Norman: University of Oklahoma Press, 1950.
I'll Die Before I'll Run. New York: Harper and Brothers, 1951.
Alias Billy The Kid (with William V. Morrison). Albuquerque: University of New Mexico Press, 1955.
Ten Texas Feuds. Albuquerque: University of New Mexico Press, 1957.
The Mescalero Apaches. Norman: University of Oklahoma Press, 1958.
Tularosa: Last Of The Frontier West. New York: Devin-Adair Company, 1960.
The El Paso Salt War. El Paso: Carl Hertzog and Texas Western Press, 1961.
The Southwest In Life And Literature: A Pageant In Seven Parts. New York: Devin-Adair Company, 1962.
Outlaw: Bill Mitchell Alias Baldy Russell. Denver: Sage Books, 1965.
Pass Of The North. El Paso: Texas Western Press, 1968
The State National Since 1881: The Pioneer Bank Of El Paso (with Millard McKinney). El Paso: Texas Western Press, 1971.
Colonel Greene And The Copper Skyrocket. Tucson: University of Arizona, 1974.
San Agustín (with George W. Chambers). Tucson: Arizona Historical Society, 1974.
From Hopalong to Hud: Thoughts On Western Fiction. College Station: Texas A.&M. University Press, 1978.
The Grave of John Wesley Hardin: Three Essays On Grassroots History. College Station: Texas A.&M. University Press, 1979.
Pass Of The North: Four Centuries On The Rio Grande Vol. 2. El Paso: Texas Western Press, 1980.
The Ambidextrous Historian: Historical Writers And Writing In The American West. Norman: University of Oklahoma Press, 1981.
Tucson: The Life And Times Of An American City. Norman: University of Oklahoma Press, 1982.

Pioneer Heritage: The First Century Of The Arizona Historical Society. Tucson: Arizona Historical Society, 1984.
Geronimo And the End Of the Apache Wars. Tucson: Arizona Historical Society, 1987.

Pilgrim in the Sun (anthology). El Paso: Texas Western Press, 1988.
The Laughing West (anthology). Athens: Ohio University Press, 1988.

Stan Steiner

Born: Brooklyn, New York, 1 January 1925.
Died: Santa Fe, New Mexico, 12 January 1987.
Career: University of Paris, associate professor. Writers Cooperative of Santa Fe, president. University of New Mexico, visiting professor. Lecturer, University of California, University of Nebraska, Colorado College, College of Idaho, University of Wyoming.
Awards: Western Writers of America, two Golden Spurs. Ansifield Wolf Award, Best Book of Race Relations. Bertrand Russell Tribunal, Honorary Jurist. *The American West* Magazine, Editorial Board, University of Paris, Best Professor of the Year.

Selected Bibliography
The New Indians. New York: Harper and Row, 1968.
La Raza: The Mexican Americans. New York: Harper Colophon Books, 1970.
The Tiguas: The Lost Tribe Of City Indians. New York: Crowell-Collier Press, 1972.
The Vanishing White Man. New York: Harper and Row, 1976.
The Ranchers: A Book Of Generations. New York: Alfred A. Knopf, 1980.
Dark And Vanishing Horsemen. San Francisco: Harper and Row, 1981.

Elizabeth Tallent

Born: Washington, D.C., 8 August 1954.
Education: Illinois State University, B.A., Anthropology, 1975.
Career: University of Southern Mississippi, writer in residence, 1983. University of California, Irvine, visiting professor, 1986.
Awards: *O. Henry Prize Short Stories.* Garden City: Doubleday, 1982. National Endowment for the Arts Fiction Fellowship, 1983. PEN Fiction Center Short Story Project, 1985.
Residence: Espanola, New Mexico.

Selected Bibliography
Married Men: John Updike's Erotic Heroes. Berkeley: Creative Arts Book Company, 1980.
In Constant Flight. New York: Alfred A. Knopf, 1983.
Museum Pieces. New York: Alfred A. Knopf, 1985.
Time With Children. New York: Alfred A. Knopf, 1987.

Luci Tapahonso

Born: Shiprock, New Mexico, 8 November 1953.
Education: University of New Mexico, B.A. Creative Writing/English, 1980; M.A. English, 1983.
Career: New Mexico Schools, artist/poet-in-the-schools, 1981-1983. University of New Mexico, Department of English, lecturer, 1982. Southwestern Indian Polytechnic Institute, Albuquerque, instructor, Language Arts, 1983. University of New Mexico, lecturer, Native American Studies, 1984-1985; assistant professor, English Department, 1985-present.
Awards: Southwest Association of Indian Affairs Literature Fellowship, 1981. University of New Mexico, Graduate English Fellowship, 1982-1983. American Book Awards, Honorable Mention, 1983.
Residence: Albuquerque, New Mexico.

Selected Bibliography

One More Shiprock Night. San Antonio: Tejas Arts Press, 1981.
Seasonal Woman. Santa Fe: Tooth of Time Press, 1982.
A Breeze Swept Through. Albuquerque: West End Press, 1987.

Sabine R. Ulibarrí

Born: Tierra Amarilla, New Mexico, 21 September 1919.
Education: University of New Mexico, B.A. University of California at Los Angeles, Ph.D.
Career: Teacher, Rio Arriba County Schools, 1938-1940; El Rito Normal, 1940-1942. United States Army Air Force, 1942-1945. University of New Mexico, professor of Modern and Classical Languages; Spanish and Spanish-American Language, Literatures and Civilization; Creative Writing, 1947-present. National Defense Education Act Language Institute, Quito, Ecuador, director, 1963, 1963. University of New Mexico Andean Center, Quito, founder and director, 1968-1969. American Association of Teachers of Spanish and Portuguese, president, 1969; member Executive Committee, 1970-1975. Academia Norteamericana de la Lengua Española, correspondent, 1978-present.
Awards: Quito, Ecuador, Distinguished Citizen, 1963; Honorary Citizen, 1964. Federation of Latin American Clubs in Europe, Award of Excellence in Promoting Hispanic Culture, 1980. New Mexico Governor's Award for Excellence in Literature, 1987.
Residence: Albuquerque, New Mexico.

Selected Bibliography

El mundo poético de Juan Ramón. Madrid, Spain: Edhigar, 1961.
Tierra Amarilla, Cuentos de Nuevo México. Quito, Ecuador: Editorial Casa de la Cultura Ecuatoriana, 1964; (bilingual edition) Albuquerque, New Mexico: University of New Mexico Press, 1971.
Al cielo se sube a pie. Madrid: Alfaguara, 1966.
Fun Learning Elementary Spanish Vol. 1. Albuquerque: University of New Mexico Department of Modern Languages, 1963.
Fun Learning Elementary Spanish Vol. II. Albuquerque: University of New Mexico Department of Modern Languages, 1965.

Madrid (translation) by Camilo Cela. Madrid: Alfaguara, 1966.
El alma de la raza. Albuquerque: University of New Mexico College of Education, 1971.
La Fragua sin fuego. Cerrillos, N. Mex.: San Marcos Press, 1971.
Mi abuela fumaba puros, My Grandmother Smoked Cigars. Berkeley: Quinto Sol, 1978.

Primeros encuentros, First Encounters. Ypsilanti, Mich.: Bilingual Press, 1982.
Pupurupú. Mexico City: Sainz Luis Elli Editores, 1987.
El gobernador Glu Glu. Tucson: Bilingual Review Press, 1987.
El cóndor, The Condor. Houston: Arte Público Press, 1988.

Frank Waters

Born: Colorado Springs, Colorado, 25 July 1902.
Education: Colorado College, Colorado Springs, Engineering, 1921-1924.
Career: Salt Creek, Wyoming, oil fields, laborer, 1924. Southern California Telephone Company, Mexican border and Los Angeles, engineer, 1925-1936. Office of Inter-American Affairs, Washington, D.C., propaganda analyist, 1943-1945. *El Crepúsculo*, weekly newspaper in Taos, New Mexico, editor, 1949-1951. Los Alamos Scientific Laboratory, Los Alamos, New Mexico, and Las Vegas, Nevada, information consultant, 1952-1956.
Awards: Honorary doctoral degrees: University of Albuquerque, Colorado State University, New Mexico State University, University of New Mexico, Colorado College, University of Colorado, University of Nevada.
Residence: Taos, New Mexico, and Tucson, Arizona.

Selected Bibliography

Fever Pitch. New York: Liveright, 1930.
The Wild Earth's Nobility. New York: Liveright, 1935.
Below Grass Roots. New York: Liveright, 1937.
Midas Of The Rockies. New York: Covici-Friede, 1937.
The Dust Within The Rock. New York: Liveright, 1940.
People Of The Valley. New York: Farrar and Rinehart, 1941.
The Man Who Killed The Deer. New York: Farrar and Rinehart, 1942.
River Lady (with Houston Branch). New York: Farrar and Rinehart, 1942.
The Colorado. New York: Rinehart and Company, 1946.
The Yogi Of Cockroach Court. New York: Rinehart and Company, 1947.
Diamond Head (with Houston Branch). New York: Farrar and Straus, 1948.
Masked Gods. Albuquerque: University of New Mexico Press, 1950.
The Earp Brothers Of Tombstone. New York: Clarkson Potter, 1960.
Book Of The Hopi. New York: Viking Press, 1963.
Leon Gaspard. Flagstaff: Northland Press, 1964.
The Woman At Otowi Crossing. Denver: Alan Swallow, 1966.
Pumpkin Seed Point. Chicago: Swallow Press, 1969.
Pike's Peak. Chicago: Swallow Press, 1969.
To Possess The Land. Chicago: Swallow Press, 1973.
Mexico Mystique. Chicago: Swallow Press, 1975.
Mountain Dialogues. Chicago: Swallow Press, 1981.
Flight From Fiesta. Santa Fe: Rydal Press, 1986.

Marta Weigle

Born: Janesville, Wisconsin, 3 July 1944.
Education: Harvard University, Radcliffe College, A.B. cum laude, Social Relations, 1965. University of Pennsylvania, M.A., Department of Folklore and Folklife, Ph.D., 1971.
Career: University of New Mexico, Albuquerque, taught English and Anthropology, 1972-present; professor of English, 1983-1987; professor of Anthropology and American Studies, 1983-present; chair, Department of American Studies, 1984-present.
Awards: For *Brothers of Light, Brothers of Blood*: State of New Mexico, Cultural Properties Review Committee, Award of Honor, 1976; University of Chicago, Chicago Folklore Prize, 1976; New Mexico Press Women, Zia Award. New Mexico Folklore Society, Roll of Honor.
Residence: Santa Fe, New Mexico.

Selected Bibliography

Follow My Fancy: The Book of Jacks and Jack Games. New York: Dover, 1970.
The Penitentes of the Southwest. Santa Fe: Ancient City Press, 1970.
Brothers of Light, Brothers of Blood: The Penitentes of the Southwest. Albuquerque: University of New Mexico Press, 1976.
A Penitente Bibliography. Albuquerque: University of New Mexico Press, 1976.
Hispano Folklife of New Mexico: The Lorin W. Brown Federal Writers' Project Manuscripts by Lorin W. Brown (edited with Charles L. Briggs). Albuquerque: University of New Mexico Press, 1978.
Spiders and Spinsters: Women and Mythology. Albuquerque: University of New Mexico Press, 1982.
Santa Fe and Taos: The Writer's Era, 1916-1941 (with Kyle Fiore). Santa Fe: Ancient City Press, 1982.
Hispanic Arts and Ethnohistory in the Southwest: New Papers Inspired by the Work of E. Boyd (edited with Claudia Larcombe and Samuel Larcombe). Albuquerque: University of New Mexico Press; Santa Fe: Ancient City Press, 1983.
Folklore/Folklife (edited with Bruce Jackson and Judith McCulloh). Washington, D.C.: American Folklore Society, 1984.
New Mexicans in Cameo and Camera: New Deal Documentation of Twentieth-Century Lives. Albuquerque: University of New Mexico Press, 1985.
Two Guadalupes: Hispanic Legends and Magic Tales From Northern New Mexico. Santa Fe: Ancient City Press, 1987.

Jeanne Williams

Born: Elkhart, Kansas, 10 April 1930.
Education: Studied professional writing with W.S. Campbell (Stanley Vestal) and William Foster-Harris at the University of Oklahoma.
Awards: Texas Institute of Letters, Best Juvenile Book, *Tame The Wild Stallion*, 1957. Levi Strauss Saddleman Award for Best Western Book of 1962. Western Writers of America Spur, *The Horse Talker*, 1962; *Freedom Trail*, 1974; *The Valiant Women*, 1980.
Residence: Cave Creek Canyon, Portal, Arizona.

Selected Bibliography

Tame the Wild Stallion. Englewood Cliffs, N.J.: Prentice-Hall, 1957.
To Buy A Dream. New York: Messner, 1958.
Promise of Tomorrow. New York: Messner, 1959.
Mission in Mexico. Englewood Cliffs, N.J.: Prentice-Hall, 1960.
The Horsetalker. Englewood Cliffs, N.J.: Prentice-Hall, 1961.
The Confederate Fiddle. Englewood Cliffs, N.J.: Prentice-Hall, 1962.
Oh, Susanna. New York: Putnam's, 1963.
Coyote Winter. New York: Norton, 1965.
Beasts With Music. New York: Meredith Press, 1967.
New Medicine. New York: Putnam's, 1972.
Trails of Tears. New York: Putnam's, 1972.
Freedom Trail. New York: Putnam's, 1973.
Winter Wheat. New York: Putnam's, 1975.
A Lady Bought With Rifles. New York: Coward, McCann and Geoghegan, 1976.
A Woman Clothed In Sun. New York: Coward, McCann and Geoghegan, 1977.
Bride of Thunder. New York: Pocket Books, 1978.
Daughter of the Sword. New York: Pocket Books, 1979.
The Valiant Women. New York: Pocket Books, 1980.
Harvest of Fury. New York: Pocket Books, 1981.
Mating of Hawks. New York: Pocket Books, 1983.
The Cave Dreamers. New York: Avon Books, 1983.
The Heaven Sword. New York: Avon Books, 1985.
So Many Kingdoms. New York: Avon Books, 1986.
Texas Pride. New York: Avon Books, 1987

As Jeanne Crecy:
Hands of Terror. New York: Berkley, 1972.
The Lightning Tree. New York: Berkley, 1973.
The Winter Keeper. New York: Signet, 1975.
The Night Hunters. New York: Signet, 1975.
My Face Beneath the Stone. New York: Signet, 1975.
The Evil Among Us. New York: Signet, 1975.

As Kristin Michaels:
To Begin With Love. New York: Signet, 1975.
Enchanted Twilight. New York: Signet, 1976.
A Special Kind of Love. New York: Signet, 1976.
Enchanted Journey. New York: Signet, 1977.
Song of the Heart. New York: Signet, 1977.
Make Believe Love. New York: Signet, 1977.
Voyage of Love. New York: Signet, 1978.
The Magic Side of the Moon. New York: Signet, 1979.

As Deirdre Rowan:
Dragon's Mount. New York: Fawcett, 1973.
Silver Wood. New York: Fawcett, 1974.
Shadow of the Volcano. New York: Fawcett, 1975.
Time of the Burning Mask. New York: Fawcett, 1976.
Ravensgate. New York: Fawcett, 1976.

As Megan Castell:
Queen of a Lonely Country. New York: Pocket Books, 1980.

As Jeanne Foster:
Deborah Leigh. New York: Fawcett, 1981.
Eden Richards. New York: Fawcett, 1982.
Woman of Three Worlds. New York: Fawcett, 1984.

Keith Wilson

Born: Clovis, New Mexico, 26 December 1927.
Education: United States Naval Academy, B.A. University of New Mexico, M.A.
Career: Naval officer, 1950-1954. University of New Mexico, 1954-1956, 1957-1958. University of Nevada, 1956-1957. Sandia Corporation, 1958-1960. University of Arizona, 1960-1965. New Mexico State University, poet-in-residence, professor of English, 1965-1987.
Awards: National Endowment for the Arts Fellowship. Senior Fulbright-Hays Fellowship. PEN-American Center Grant. D.H. Lawrence Creative Writing Fellowship. Nominated, National Book Award, *While Dancing Feet Shatter The Earth.*
Residence: Las Cruces, New Mexico.

Selected Bibliography

Sketches For A New Mexico Hill Town. Orono, Maine: Wine Press, 1967.
II Sequences. Orono, Maine: Wine Press, 1967.
The Old Car. La Grande, Oreg.: Grande Ronde Press, 1967.
Graves Registry And Other Poems. New York: Grove Press, 1969.
Homestead. San Francisco: Kayak Press, 1969.
Rocks. Oshkosh, Wis.: Roadrunner Press, 1971.
The Shadow Of Our Bones. Portland, Oreg.: Trask House Books, 1971.
The Old Man And Others: Some Faces For America. Las Cruces: New Mexico State University, 1971.
Psalms For Various Voices. Las Cruces, N. Mex.: Tolar Creek Press, 1972.
Midwatch. Fremont, Mich.: Sumac Press, 1972.
Thantog: Songs Of A Jaguar Priest. Dennis, Mass.: Saltworks Press, 1977.
The Shaman Deer. Dennis, Mass.: Saltworks Press, 1979.
While Dancing Feet Shatter The Earth. Logan, Utah: Utah State University Press, 1978.
Desert Cenote. Fort Kent, Maine: Great Raven Press, 1978.
The Streets Of San Miguel. Tucson: Maguey Press, 1977.
Retablos. Cerrillos, N. Mex.: San Marcos Press, 1980.
Stone Roses: Poems From Transylvania. Logan, Utah: Utah State University Press, 1983.
Meeting In Jal (with Theodore Enslin). Hobbs, N. Mex.: Hawk Press, 1985.
Lion's Gate: Selected Poems 1963-1968. El Paso: Cinco Puntos Press, 1987.

Norman Zollinger

Born: Chicago, Illinois, 8 November 1921.
Education: Cornell College, Mt. Vernon, Illinois.
Career: Manufacturing executive until 1971. Bookseller, 1971-present.
Awards: Western Writers of America, Golden Spur, and Border Regional Library Association Award for *Riders To Cibola*, 1978.
Residence: Albuquerque, New Mexico.

Selected Bibliography

Riders To Cibola. Santa Fe: Museum of New Mexico Press, 1977.
Corey Lane. New Haven: Ticknor and Fields, 1981.

Ann Zwinger

Born: Muncie, Indiana.

Education: Wellesley College, B.A., Art History, 1946. Indiana University, M.A., Art History, 1950. Radcliffe College, Ph.D. residence, Art History, 1951-1952. Colorado College, studied entomology, plant morphology, field botany, printmaking, 1963-1964, 1978-1980.

Career: Smith College, instructor, Art History, 1950-1951. University of Kansas, 1958-1960. Benet Hill Academy, Colorado Springs, 1963-1965. Colorado College, guest lecturer, 1973-1981, visiting faculty, 1987. Director, American Electric Power, 1977-present.

Awards: Nominee, National Book Award in Science, *Land Above the Trees*, 1973. John Burroughs Association Award, *Run, River, Run*, 1976. Friends of American Writers Award for Nonfiction, *Run, River, Run*, 1976. Colorado College, Doctor of Humane Letters, 1976. Wellesley College Alumnae Award, 1976. Garden Clubs of America, Sara Chapman Francis Medal, 1977. Carleton College, Doctor of Humane Letters, 1984. Colorado Author's Guild, Adult Nonfiction Award, *A Desert Country Near the Sea*, 1984.

Residence: Colorado Springs, Colorado.

Selected Bibliography

Beyond The Aspen Grove. New York: Random House, 1970.

Land Above The Trees (with Dr. Beatrice E. Willard). New York: Harper and Row, 1971.

Run, River, Run. New York: Harper and Row, 1975.

Wind In The Rock. New York: Harper and Row, 1977.

A Conscious Stillness (with Edwin Way Teale). New York: Harper and Row, 1982.

A Desert Country Near The Sea. New York: Harper and Row, 1983.

Xántus: The Letters Of John Xántus To Spencer Fullerton Baird From San Francisco And Cabo San Lucas, 1859-1861. Los Angeles: Dawson's Bookshop, 1986.

John Xántus: The Fort Tejon Letters, 1857-1859. Tucson: University of Arizona Press, 1986.

Colorado II (with David Muench). Portland, Oreg.: Graphic Arts Center Publishing Company, 1987.

Recipient of the 1987
C.L. Sonnichsen Book Award
Texas Western Press
of The University of Texas at El Paso

Designed by Kathleen Rogers
Text set in Oracle
Display set in Papyrus
Duotone negatives by Sunset Color Graphics

Special thanks to
Southwestern Bell Telephone
for its gift in support of this book's publication